GUIDE TO WRITING & PUBLISHING

SCIENCE FICTION

FANTASY

HORROR

by

Rob Shelsky

* * * * *

Guide To Writing & Publishing
Science Fiction
Fantasy
Horror

PUBLISHED BY:

GKRS PUBLICATIONS
ISBN-13: 978-1461184119
ISBN-10: 1461184118

Copyright © 2011 by Rob Shelsky

This is a work of nonfiction. The author acknowledges the trademarked status and trademark owners of any products referenced in this work of nonfiction, which have been used without permission. The publication/use of these trademarks is not authorized, associated with, or sponsored by the trademark owners. All quotations and/or related materials are referenced either in the body of this book itself, or referenced in Appendix I at the end.

There is one person I'd especially like to thank,
because I owe him so much:

George Kempland; I wish to acknowledge you
for your loyalty, dedication, mountains of help, and
always just being there for me.

Again, thank you so very much, now and always.

* * * * *

GUIDE TO WRITING & PUBLISHING

SCIENCE FICTION

FANTASY

HORROR

By

Rob Shelsky

TABLE OF CONTENTS

INTRODUCTION
How To Get Published!

To write and get published—now that's the whole point here! The idea is to get your work published as a science fiction, fantasy, or horror author, and as quickly as possible! That's the reason for my writing this book and certainly it is the primary motivation for you, as an author, to read it, to obtain the knowledge you need to get your books "out there." And this is going to be a daring topic, because the title makes it sound as if I actually know what I'm talking about here.

Well, actually, I do know exactly what I'm talking about! I have been repeatedly published and at professional rates, and I do have three novels and three anthologies out, as well as two nonfiction works. They're all selling well. Besides these, my writing credits include numerous published short stories and many factual articles for a multitude of different magazines. (Please see, **Author's Note.**) I've been a resident columnist on science fiction with **AlienSkin Magazine** for the better part of seven years, as well. So trust me, when I say I'm well versed on the subject of how to get published.

And this book is a synthesis, a compilation of articles I've written over those seven years concerning all aspects of these two subjects, writing and publishing. These articles all of have been published for good money. And that's what you, as a writer, want to do—get published and for good money!

Here, I've arranged the articles in a logical progression, so that all aspects of writing in the genres of science fiction, fantasy, and horror are covered in a cohesive, step-by-step manner.

We start with the basics of getting published, then elaborate on how we get ideas for a story, develop settings for those ideas, create plots, incorporate themes, etc.

Why have I included the three genres of science fiction, horror, and fantasy here together? Because they have so much in common, and so often cross over. One can have pure horror, but as with Stephen King, often it is more a form of science fiction horror (think *Tommy Knockers*, *Dreamcatcher*, etc.). The same holds true for fantasies. So often, they can be set in alternate realities, but still here on Earth, or on other worlds where they really are science fiction masquerading as fantasies.

Not to mention the reverse is often true. I've always felt that the *Dragon Rider* series by Anne McCaffrey was more fantasy than science fiction. Andre Norton, with her post-apocalyptic novels, often crossed the genres to some degree. Horror, again, often has science fiction as a strong element in it, or even fantasy (vampires, werewolves, banshees, ghosts, etc.). So fantasy, horror, and science fiction all have strong, basic, and common elements. All three of these genres are very close in style and substance when it comes to settings, plots, pace, suspense, and such. So it follows that the five steps to getting published are the same for all three of these genres.

Once we've covered these steps, then we move on to other practical aspects of writing. For example, what does it take to create a good horror story? What are the primary conditions for writing a successful one? How do we design our fantasy world so that it's believable to the readers? What's the difference between hard and soft science fiction? Can we use faster-than-light travel in hard science fiction tales? Do editors want stories about UFOs still? Is time travel now a passé subject for stories? Are Steampunk and cross-genres stories the wave of the future? Have vampires run their course? How about werewolves? What exactly is "mundane science fiction?" That genre is getting very popular, you know. How does one develop a writing style, find a distinctive voice in the crowded field of writing? Why it is that suddenly some subject is so popular, while others aren't?

Then, finally, we will move on to the more esoteric aspects of writing in these genres, such as whether we authors get to comment on how and whether we should incorporate our personal opinions on such various subjects as religion, political viewpoints, society's ills, global warming, consumer societies—

well, you get the idea. For instance, does religion have any place in our genres? Is science fiction, fantasy, or horror at all about warning readers of possible future scenarios that are dangerous for us all? What of self-censorship? What do we dare write and when, and how far do we dare go?

The answers to all these questions and many more are all here in these pages—just about everything and anything you'd care to know about how to get published in any of these genres, and how to write those stories editors will want to buy. The steps are easy and they will almost certainly work if followed!

What brought this need for the steps to getting published (outlined in the first chapter to my attention? Well, I belonged to an organization known as Critters.org. This free organization allows science fiction, horror, and fantasy writers to submit their stories to the group and then to have them reviewed by other writers there, and for free! It's quite a valuable asset for authors, really, because rather than getting the stories reviewed and rejected by editors (who won't want to see that particular story ever again), it allows authors to first work out the kinks in their tales before even submitting them through a peer-group, review process. This means a greater chance of a successful submission first time around for the authors who do this. And that's what it's all about—getting your submissions accepted. So peer group review is a great idea. Again, it truly helps when it comes to avoiding rejections from those hard-to-please editors.

But here's another and even more important reason why I mention Critters.org; I've found in reviewing other authors' stories there, that more often than not, they are missing some of the most necessary and basic ingredients required to getting their stories published. So since this seems to be such a common problem with so many authors, I thought we could go over those items here. **This plan works for any genre of fiction writing, whether fantasy, horror, science fiction, slipstream, romance, mystery, adventure, women's fiction, literary—you name it!** The steps are so basic, it works for them all. However, this book is aimed primarily at authors of science fiction, fantasy, and horror/paranormal.

And no, you don't need seven steps, or ten, or whatever, in order to get published, and as so many new authors like to say on their blog sites. Five will do just fine. We will enumerated these five steps to getting published and we will discuss each in depth, as well as other facets of writing in these genres—how to write them better, and different ways to do this.

In short, we'll cover just about every aspect of writing, from how to write, to what to write, to how to get published, with tips on all sorts of subjects included to make the job easier for you, as an author. So are you ready for the five basic steps to getting published? Well, here goes!

CHAPTER 1

Five Easy Steps To Getting A Story Published

Unlike so many books, which wait until the very end to give you what you need to know to actually get published (and this is done just to make you read the whole thing), I'm going to tell you right up front, here in the very first chapter, the five steps involved in getting successfully published. Here they are:

STEP 1. Come up with an idea for a story and then open it with a hook! First, you have to have an idea for a story, of course. This can come from anywhere, other books, and movies, something in your own life or someone else's life, a photograph or painting, something on the television may be your inspiration—ideas for stories can just about come from anywhere, any source. One of the easiest ways is to steal an idea. Yes, sounds wrong, doesn't it? But not the way we go about it here.

Mind you, you aren't actually and blatantly stealing an idea. But we'll get to this with an in-depth look at how to go about getting ideas in the next chapter. For right now, we'll assume you already have an idea, because you want to write a book, and who would want to do that if they didn't have an idea of what they wanted to write? Right?

So the first thing an author must remember is that *the tale must open with a hook!* This is essential. Endlessly, I've pointed this out to would-be writers. Most either don't bother to listen, or don't seem to "get" just what a hook really is. So, I thought I'd explain it here. A hook is actually a headliner of sorts, an attention-getting device, a "grabber" if you will. There are thousands of stories out there, so what is it that makes a reader want to pick your story out of the crowd? Why, it's the hook, of course!

You, as an author, have about three sentences, or at the most, a small paragraph at the very beginning of your story, in which to grab your reader's attention and make him/her want to read more. *If you* **don't** *hook the reader right away, you have already lost them forever! You simply must grab and then hold their attention at the outset.*

Perhaps, even more important than the reader's attention, is those editors' interest. If you can seize their attention for your story, amidst a slush pile of hundreds or thousands of submissions that they have to wade through, then you have already won half the battle. You see, they will actually then go on to read your story, and not just glance at it and toss it aside for a rejection slip.

So what are some examples of excellent hooks? Here are just a few:

"The sleet arrived on the wind that howled out of the Firgeberg, gray particles that abraded skin, stung eyes.

—C.J. Cherryth, Cloud Rider, Chapter 1, opening lines.

Or:

"Tatya raised herself on one elbow and gaped through the sleeping-room port at the night sky, her china-blue eyes wide. She hadn't imagined it.

—Margaret Wander Bonanno, Star Trek Stranger From The Sky, Chapter 1, opening lines.

Or:

"Durvash the tnuctipun knew he was dying. The thought did not bother him overmuch—he was a warrior of a peculiar and desperate kind and had never expected to survive the War—but the consciousness of failure was far worse than the wound along his side."

—Larry Niven, S.M. Stirling, Thomas T. Thomas, Man-Kzin Wars V, opening lines of prologue.

See how a hook works? These accomplished authors, with just a sentence or two, set a scene, created tension, and often characters were introduced, as well. And all this was done in just one or two lines! Most importantly, the writers create a sort of mystery for their reader as to what is coming next. This makes the reader wants to know more. That's the hook, the "grabber," if you will. Your story must absolutely start with one of these if you want it to be published. Without a hook, you've already failed in this endeavor.

STEP 2. A beginning, middle, and an end. This may sound incredibly obvious, but believe me, it doesn't seem to be for many authors. Writers, both male and female, will often lovingly create scenarios that they seem to fall in love with themselves. They will painstakingly paint in characters, backgrounds, whole lifestyles, and then have something happen. But often there is no opening and no resolution. It's as if the reader has just stumbled into something after it's already started, glimpsed something in passing. We, as readers, catch a quick look at something that could be a story, and then it's over—no resolution. It ends up being just one scene, a scenario, or a vignette, and not a story at all.

Avoid this pitfall! Remember, your story must have a real beginning, middle, and an end that resolves whatever tension/dilemma the story has created. Pace and plot are everything. That which does not further your plot should be taken out! So editing is crucial. It's been said that when you think you have the perfect story in every detail, then you should edit (cut) it by another ten to fifteen percent. Sounds, cruel, but if you don't do it, editors will. And it makes a better impression on them if they don't have to tell you to do this. The mark of a good author is to know when his story needs cutting, and that's hard, because we think every word of our books is worth keeping, don't we? And that's why peer-group reviews help so. Others will spot weaknesses that as the author of the work, you are blind to, or just don't want to see.

Have you ever read a novel where you breezed over whole paragraphs, because they were too pedantic, said too little, and didn't add much to the plot? You were in a hurry to see what comes next. We all have done this. So, you don't want this as an author to happen to you. You want your readers to hang on every word, if you can. And that's where that final round of tough cutting comes in. And if you don't do it, again, your editor will. Trust me! That is, if they don't find the pace so slow that they reject the book outright.

STEP 3. Willing suspension of disbelief, believable hero(ine)s, tension and resolution. Yeah, yeah, this one gets pounded to death, but there is a reason for that; it's important—incredibly important! Your story must allow the reader to suspend their disbelief for the duration of reading it, to believe that what takes place in the story is actually possible under the circumstances and conditions given. Your characters and plot must come across as real to them, at least for the duration of time they are reading your book.

People have to be able to identify with the main character, care about what is happening to him/her. And finally, the tension must reach a satisfactory resolution (satisfactory for the reader that is). "To be continued…" may work for television shows, but it is not popular when someone has bought a $30.00 book, only to find it's really just half a book and leaves them hanging! Nothing is worse, in my estimation, than reading hundreds of pages just to find out that absolutely nothing or little is resolved! It is my firm belief that even with books that form a series, each volume should tell a whole story, one that is complete in itself, even though the main theme may continue on to the next book. The *Harry Potter* books by J.K. Rowling do this quite nicely, for example.

As always, make sure you keep a decent pace going in your story. Don't let it bog down or drag in parts, because the reader will lose interest and may not finish reading the tale. How do you avoid this negative outcome? Again, you must edit your story. Edit, edit, and edit it some more! As previously mentioned (and it can't be said enough) It's said that the average story, when finished by the author, and believed to be in its best possible state by them, should then be cut by another ten to fifteen percent minimum! Sounds harsh, doesn't it? But such editing does wonders for the pace of a story.

Besides maintaining a good pace, a writer must keep titillating the reader's interest. Each chapter or scene should end, just as the hook should, with the reader wanting to know "what's coming next?" And remember that your hero should either win through after almost being defeated, or go down in flames in the pursuit of a nobler cause, something worthwhile for them dying for, something greater by far than they are as an individual. Why do this? Nobody likes a loser, that's why! And remember, if your characters, setting, or plot comes across as unbelievable, your willing suspension of disbelief is lost, and then you'll quickly lose the reader's interest. You don't want that! We will discuss more on how to maintain willing suspension of disbelief in later chapters.

STEP 4. Submit Your Story! No pun intended here, but now "this one is really for the books" (okay—I intended that pun), because I am often astonished at how many people will write short stories and novels, and then never quite "get around" to submitting them to a publisher/editor, so that they can become an actual "book." What's the point then of doing all that hard writing work? I know it isn't easy to send one's "baby" in to some strange publisher, one who will probably treat it badly, and find all sorts of fault with it, but it is necessary to submit your work. If the editor loves it—great, you're in! If he/she hates it—well, at least you know you have more work to do.

And remember to always do and send your best work, not "first drafts." Treat editors with respect. Give them the kind of thing you'd want to get—that is, something clean, neat, readable, and without many typos and/or other errors. Most of us have spelling and grammar checkers now. For heaven's sake, use them! Otherwise, your work will look unprofessional, and you will seem inept as a writer, and so probably a poor author. First impressions are important in writing! And your submission is the editor's first impression of you. If it's a bad first impression, good luck getting published!

And yes, it's always hard to face rejection. So, it's perfectly okay to retreat into your personal womb, to comfort yourself and hate the editor for a while—a little while. So eat those chocolates. Pull down that shade and huddle in bed for a bit. But then you have to get over it, straighten out of that fetal position, stop sucking your thumb, and get a move on. Read your story once more with an eye to improvements. Make changes to your tale and then send it out again! And again, and again, and again, until you get it published! "Persistence" is the key word here, folks. It's an absolute must. Even if your story is great, some editors simply won't want it. That's life. So you must keep submitting your work until you find an editor that does like it.

Start with those publications that pay the best and work your way down the list from there. Two good sites (among others) for finding markets for your stories, if they are in the science fiction, horror, or fantasy genres are *Ralan's Webstravaganza*, and *The Spicy Green Iguana*. Both are well maintained and are very up to date on which markets are dead, so you don't waste your time on sending your work to dead "zines." These are both free sites, with direct links to various publications, and descriptions of what each of those publishers want.

But now back to those editors—there is one other alternative an editor might do that can really help you, and that leads us to our next and last step.

STEP 5. If an editor gives you a rejection, but one with editorial advice, use it! Again, I know it's hard to have to take rejection. Even after all this time, I still hate it, and I'm always highly suspicious of any editor that doesn't realize just how valuable and WONDERFUL my work really is! We all think that. Right? And being writers, we're all sensitive souls, too. This makes it even hard to take such criticism. But if you get an editor who tells you what they think is wrong with your work, than you are so lucky! Take their advice. Consider it carefully and then make the appropriate changes. And if an editor hasn't done this for you, there are always those critique groups, such as Critters.org, you can join as a substitute. But constructive criticisms from editors are like gold—incredibly valuable to you as a writer, and to improving your work.

So often with the reviews I do of people's stories, I get thank-you letters that although polite, will push the fact that the author doesn't agree with what I've said, and therefore, is going to stand by the way they've already written their story, and not change it. That's fine with me. It's an author's prerogative. But…SEE YA! And that's probably what an editor will say if you give them that kind of response to their critique of your work.

Understand this: if an editor bothers to tell you just what they feel is wrong with your work, then they are trying to help you. Get it? They aren't being mean just for the heck of it. They have nothing to gain. On the contrary, doing this takes up valuable time for them. So they are truly granting you an honor—some of that precious time.

Treat it as such. Act on it. Understand that they have no stake in helping you, other than the fact that they want to, probably think that your writing quality is worth their help, and so can benefit from it. But if you don't agree with them, and insist on getting on your high horse, then I have a suggestion for you: take that horse and ride on out of town! Go straight to the land of denial. Nobody will care, I tell you, least of all editors or publishers.

If you don't like or can't abide the responses you might get, then don't send the stories out at all! Don't write! The whole point is to get your tale published, or at least get feedback, to know how to revise, and write a better version so you can then get it published. Otherwise, what's the point of being an author? Unpublished authors are a dime a dozen. Would-be writers fill the world. It's only those authors who actually write and submit their work who have a chance of seeing it in print, of getting paid.

Honestly, I sometimes wonder what some writers do want—just a smug pat on the back, and to be told how great they are? Forget that! You can get all the reassurance you need from your mommy or daddy! What an author needs is cold, hard, clear advice on how to improve their work and then use it to get published!

One valid point though; the author does and should always have the final say on their story. That's as it should be. But use that power wisely, little grasshoppers! Don't let ego get in the way of writing a better story, one that can get published!

And there you have it. If you've done these five easy steps correctly, you'll get a story accepted—right? Yes, you will, but maybe not right away. Some editors have their own personal biases and simply may not like your style, the topic, characters, etc. Others may like the story, but have already accepted something too similar. This has happened to me. Still other editors may like your story, but just not feel it is right for their magazine.

That can't be helped. We are all individuals and people have their own set feelings about things, even editors. So again, be persistent; keep sending your story out there. Make sure you are sending it to the right venue for your particular genre. Many writers make that simple mistake—picking the wrong publication for their work, or just sending it to a few before giving up and shelving their story. But trust me, do these steps properly and eventually your story will find a home.

I will tell you that following this advice will markedly and I mean **MARKEDLY**, increase your chances of being published soon, and often! You will get published by using these methods. You see, I'm not the first to come up with these steps. Practically every successful author has learned them either on their own, or from someone else, just as I have. I wish I could claim rights to them, but I can't.

And now that we have the basic steps for getting published taken care of, let's move on to discussing in depth how we should actually write our stories. We need to know such things as what are the requirements to create horror, how to create realistic settings for science fiction, what topics are appropriate to write about in fantasy, and so much more! In the following section, we will discuss how to get ideas for our science fiction, fantasy, and horror novels. Do remember, these same principles apply to most other types of fiction works, as well, whether historical, literary, women's fiction, or whatever. So let's see how we get our ideas for what we want to write! We'll start with those in the very next chapter.

CHAPTER 2

The Fine Art Of Stealing Ideas—An Age-Old Tradition

"Don't worry about people stealing your ideas. If your ideas are any good, you'll have to ram them down people's throats."

—Howard Aiken

Question: Mr. (Ray) Bradbury, what is the best way to learn to write?

Answer: "Read. Read everything you can and read often. To be a good science fiction writer, or any kind of writer for that matter, you must learn by example. And reading other author's works, will give you ideas that you can steal. I don't mean to steal them in the literal sense, but you will see ideas that you like, can then develop, and eventually make your own. All authors do this."

Is this an exact quote of Ray Bradbury's? No, not exactly, because it's been a long time since I heard it, but this is how I remember him answering when I once asked him about the best way to learn to write science fiction, how to go about learning to write in general, actually. And believe me; my memory of this is pretty darn clear, because I idolized Ray Bradbury and wanted to write just as he and other great science fiction writers of the time did, such as Isaac Asimov, Robert Heinlein, Theodore Sturgeon, Andre Norton, and so many others.

So, stealing ideas for stories, that is in the sense of taking them, massaging them, and making them into your own, is a time-honored institution in the genre of science fiction, horror, and fantasy, and many other genres, as well.

Don't believe me? Well, how about this comment attributed to Isaac Asimov:

> *"As a matter of fact...if one SF writer thinks up something which is very useful, another may put it into his own words and use it freely. Nobody in SF is going to accuse any other person in SF of using his ideas; in fact, we borrow so generously that there's no way of telling whose idea it was originally."*

So there you have it. Right from the biggest of the big, you've been told—they all steal ideas. And many authors have used Isaac Asimov's Three Laws of Robotics, just as he says. Mr. Asimov was certainly right about that aspect of things. Even on **Star Trek Next Generation**, Data, the android, had a "positronic" brain, which is a direct steal from Isaac's own novels. Of course, this was undoubtedly done as a tribute, and a fine one it was, too.

And no, let's make this clear right now, we do not mean you should actually just out-and-out steal ideas. We are not talking plagiarism here. Rather, you should take an idea that intrigues you, work it, remold it, reshape it, and thus make it your own. Again, as Mr. Asimov says, *"we inhabit a small, specialized world,"* and this is very true of us science fiction writers. Some might even say we are almost intellectually incestuous in this regard, because we do form close-knit bonds with our fellow writers of science fiction, fantasy, and horror. Stealing ideas, I suppose, is an inevitable outcome of this.

So, how exactly do we go about this, this stealing of an idea and creating our own unique story out of it? Well, do what Ray Bradbury suggested. Read. Read a lot! Read and absorb, and certain ideas will hit you and spark your interest. These you may want to work on more. For me, one big issue was and still is for that matter, immortality. To get an idea of how we steal ideas and make them our own, let's follow how I evolved a single story based on a sort of stolen idea. It's the best way I can think of to show a straightforward example:

First Step: <u>Steal an idea</u>. I'd read a short story once that so intrigued me, it made me stop and think about immortality. But, of course, I didn't want to simply rewrite someone else's story, not even "in my own words." That would be tantamount to plagiarism, in any case. I wanted what I wrote to be my own! So I thought about immortality some more. And the question arose for me; what would be the social outcome if the majority of humanity wanted everlasting life, but the few didn't? Then I extended this idea to having it be indigenous people, in, say, Australia and North America, who for their own reasons rejected immortality.

Now you have two groups, an advanced species of humanity tantamount to aliens, and another, following the traditional morals and precepts of their ancestors. One more thing; add to this that the immortals could still die by accident, in plane wrecks, explosions, etc. The answer to this for me was that they would want to avoid this. They would become a very conservative species, disinclined to take chances, but not quite as we might imagine this. The advanced race, in my story, decided to leave Earth (it being a relatively unsafe place to live, what with volcanoes, earthquakes, tsunamis, hurricanes, and all), so the question arises: where would they go that was safer?

Second Step: <u>Steal another idea</u>. My people, like Asimov's people of earth, would retreat to *Caves of Steel*, but not on earth, it being just too dangerous. They would go to the asteroids, hollow them out. Here, with the help of robotics, they could live in relative safety. An iron-nickel shell around them, virtually infinite resources from the Oort Cloud and Kuiper Belt, plus the resources of the whole asteroid belt. With their technology, avoiding collisions, etc., would be no problem. Here, without having to rely on the sun's power to survive, and in fact avoiding dangerous solar flares this way, they could endure for millions, perhaps even billions of years.

Third Step: <u>Steal yet another idea</u>! Now, what if the advanced race, in departing, is stricken with guilt at the last moment. How can they leave a portion of humanity behind, subject to old age, disease, and death? Well, you can't force adults to leave against their will in an enlightened society. That would be just wrong. But children not of legal age are subject to the State's authority. The State can decide what's best for them, despite what the parents might wish, and in my story they did just this. They resolve to take all the children of Earth; leaving the adults behind, if they so wish it. Sound familiar to some degree? Think Arthur C. Clarke's, *Childhood's End*. Remember when the aliens came and the children were changed, no longer able to relate to their parents, but in the process became part of a much greater intelligence? See how this idea stealing works? You take ideas, massage them, and incorporate them. In the process, you are synthesizing a new "whole."

Fourth Step: <u>Steal one more idea</u>. Yep, I'm that bad! I did it yet again. It wasn't enough to have the grand sweep of events as my story. I had to personalize it, bring it down to the human scale. So I did what every famous author, as well as practically every author does, for that matter. I made it relate to the reader on an individual level. I focused on just two people, a Native Australian father and son. But I reversed the roles (my own idea—at long last). I made the father more inclined to be liberal and like the "Golden Ones," those immortal beings, while the teenage son hated them and was more conservative, not wanting change to come in any way. The interaction of these two, what they had to deal with when facing forced separation, and the outcome, may not be what you thought!

Did this stealing of ideas work? You betcha! The story was published at professional rates in **Jim Baen's Universe Magazine**, now sadly, recently closed (I hope not because of my story…).

So there you have it. Stealing ideas can be a good thing. It's highly accepted and always has been in the science fiction world. The important thing here is to remember that you are just stealing an idea, or in my case, ideas. You must make them your own. Evolve them, develop them, and change until they not only reflect you, but truly are yours. Again, even for a single story, this may involve even more than one such idea. This way, you have created a new whole that is greater than the sum of those parts, those original ideas. And guess what; if you do it well enough, someone may very well steal ideas from your story! That's the way of things, and that's a good thing. We live, we learn, and we grow. And hopefully, as those science fiction greats have done, we pass something on to the next generation of authors.

And one last thing I thought I should mention; I didn't just get one story about immortality out of this. I ended up with two, both published. See what I mean? Stealing ideas isn't just an age-old tradition; it's also a profitable one! So how do we come up with ideas if we can't find one to steal and rework to make our own? Well, the next chapter deals with this problem.

CHAPTER 3

How To Come Up With Fresh Ideas For Plots

"Ideas are like rabbits. You get a couple and learn how to handle them, and pretty soon you have a dozen of them."
—John Steinbeck

"How do you come up with such weird ideas?" I usually get that question when I read a story aloud to some cornered friend (one usually desperate to escape from my literary clutches—it's true—I've seen their fingernail scratches on my front and back doors—very sad). Not, "Wow, what a great idea!" or "Gee, that's a cool story." Nope. Just, "How do you come up with such weird ideas?" Oh well, at least I may become famous for something someday, if only "weird ideas," or maybe not!

But, let's not denigrate the usefulness of any such ability. One of the hardest things to do in today's crowded writing market is not so much to write a good story, so much as it is to write one that hasn't been done a thousand times before. Don't believe it? Well then, check out editors' guidelines on the Internet and elsewhere. They (editors), usually don't want any stories about UFO's, time travel, werewolves, vampires, etc. Now, not all say this, of course. Some editors specifically want these sorts of subjects (the minority of editors), and for their particular magazines, but even there, they are careful to say that it must be more than just the same old trite stuff they've received a thousand times before. In others words, for many topics, editors are crying loudly and clearly that: **IT'S BEEN DONE!**

So, let's say you consider yourself a fair or even good writer, one able to develop a plot, but the trouble is you just can't seem to come up with a truly original idea for one. Well then, how does one go about trying to do just that? How does an author come up with something unique, entirely new, or at least with a definite fresh twist to it? Is this easy to do, especially when everyone is saying that there "is nothing new under the sun" in the science fiction, horror, and fantasy genres left for them to write? In other words, how do you, as a science fiction or horror writer, manage to make your work stand out in a huge crowd?

Well, first let's clarify the issue by restating the exact nature of the problem once more:

1. The problem is how to come up with new/fresh ideas for plots.

Why is that so hard for so many of us? Perhaps, it may be because we all tend to think within the boundaries of our own genres. In other words, if we're writing horror and we're trying to come up with an idea, we almost automatically dwell on ideas about creepy monsters, vampires, werewolves, zombies, Cthulu-like creatures, things in the cellar, etcetera, and etcetera. If it's science fiction we're writing, we equally automatically think about end-of-the-world scenarios, aliens, spacecraft, first contact, time travel, and such. Why? I think it's because these topics, loosely, tend to form our genres, or that's how authors perceive the situation. These timeworn topics define, encapsulate, and even dictate what we write, the contents and boundaries of our genres. They form and label what type of authors we are.

In others words, we've inadvertently put ourselves in a box. Yes, it is one only defined by our readers, certainly, and ourselves primarily, but just as real, just as limiting, nevertheless. Over time, we authors have developed strict boundaries for that imaginary box, what we think it should contain. Any crossover and we're suddenly not science fiction writers anymore, or at least that's what we think!

2. A solution to the problem for coming up with new ideas for plots; can you get out of that box?

If our own boundaries define what topics are okay to be included in our particular genre box, then they also exclude, as a matter of course, numerous topics that would be labeled as being "outside of the box." So, possible solutions to our problem of coming up with fresh new ideas for stories are therefore denied to us. This isn't a new concept by any means. The corporate world has been promoting and propounding this philosophy in an ongoing effort to get their employees to be more imaginative when it comes to solving business problems. They actively try to get their managers to think beyond self-imposed limitations in order to find new answers, new solutions, and ones that might not ever have even been considered before.

3. Exactly how do we go about getting out of the box?

The answer to that might be easier than you think! You simply have to redefine what the limitations of your box are. Make it bigger, or get rid of it all together. Science fiction was created by writers. Again, we've defined it. Readers developed a taste for what we wrote, and that was our feedback. Using what readers like, we wrote more on the same subjects—something of a vicious circle, it seems. And although this is a normal process when seeking success (building on what's already been done and even replicating it), it is a self-limiting one. So, just think about challenging yourself and your readers. Give them something new to read, something new about which to think.

How? Start by taking a pad and pen, laptop, Ipad, or blackberry/PDA, or whatever technical trappings trip your trigger. Take whichever of these things suits you best with you wherever you go. Whenever an idea occurs to you about anything as a plot, jot it down right then. This could happen in a store, bar, a park, bark, at work (don't let the boss catch you though), or anywhere. Keep adding more ideas to your lists. If you wake up from a strange dream some morning, one that left you feeling as if it were truly bizarre, it might make for the germ of an idea for a good story.

I once had a dream about meteors destroying a city. Out of that dream, came the plot line for my *Bradbury County*, which is now a published story, and coming out in a hardcover anthology soon, along with works by some very famous authors, such as Alastair Reynolds and Mary Rosenblum, among many others. So, don't discount even your dreams as sources of plot lines. I should think horror stories could evolve from nightmares very well, since they come from the subconscious, where all our darkest fears and desires dwell.

So, keep jotting down such ideas. I can't stress this enough. Later, you can review them to see if any of them still hold value as possible future plots for you. Ideas can come from anywhere if you just open yourself up to them. For instance, you might be watching a horse show on some cable channel. Then, you might wonder what aliens would think about horses, or how someone on an isolated horse ranch might confront something from another plane of existence. A horse ranch in the middle of nowhere makes for a perfect horror setting.

Or, have you ever noticed all the RV's on the roads these days? What if they aren't just retired people going to and from Florida? What if they actually form a secret, mobile society? Perhaps, it is one with dark goals, and only their own members are privy to this information? Conspiracy theories anyone? This could make for a great serious, comedic, or ironic tale.

Of course, some of the ideas you come up with just won't work. However, if you note down all your ideas and concepts on a regular basis, the result of this note taking will be at least some plausible possibilities for plots. Think about their merits, their drawbacks, and if they'd make for something original and fresh. Then, work with them, write something about them, and see if you like the results.

Another approach is to fasten on some mundane thing, and then try to approach it from some truly novel way. Examples? Well, let's say you're viewing a portrait of Henry VIII, that Tudor tyrant. Think about him a little differently. What if his life and times weren't so cut and dried? What if some alien or time traveler helped him to achieve such supremacy? What if he wasn't from his own time, but an interloper, a changeling, or a puppet of some higher power? Or, how about two atomic clocks on the wall, and the main character of the tale notices each of them showing a differing time display, say, a discrepancy of just a few minutes? What could account for this anomaly? You see? Fresh ideas can crop up in the strangest places, at any time, and under any conditions.

Stephen King did this sort of thing well. He took such mundane things as cars, trucks, cats—you name it, and wove fanciful horror stories out of them. And they've been big hits with readers every since, not to mention movie goers! And don't be afraid to borrow from other genres. Here's an example—come up with a sound and practical reason for a horde of werewolves besieging a science station on an alien planet. Heaven knows that horror borrows heavily from science fiction, so why not work the reverse more than we tend to do now. And do you ever watch the new episodes of Doctor Who? They come up with explanations (reasonably believable sometimes), for everything from witches in Elizabethan England, to werewolves hunting Queen Victoria. The possibilities, to use a cliché, are endless.

So, approach your subject matter as if it had no limitations on what it can include. Don't be afraid to mix and match genres, but do always pay attention to the rules. If it's science fiction, you'd better have a reasonable explanation for all those werewolves! Heck, they could even be artificial, being androids, or robotic in nature, but there has to be a plausible-sounding explanation. If horror or fantasy, again, you have to have reasonable suspension of disbelief still, so that means having reasonable explanations for what's happening in your tale.

In conclusion on this topic, let me just say again that if you want new or fresh ideas and twists on tired topics, then seek out new sources in the mundane. Go beyond your self-imposed limitations and see the obvious in the not so obvious way. Try to look at the common in a completely new light. Approach things from a new perspective and fresh ideas are sure to follow. After all, playing with the mundane world worked for Stephen King and many others. So why shouldn't it work for you? It can you know, if you just allow yourself to entertain the possibilities.

Need some examples? Well, let's take global warming as just one possible topic.

This is a subject I can really warm up to despite its chilling implications. (Yes, another pun…) First, let's face it square on; global warming is here. It is real. Yes, I know some scientists still quibble over that, but they are the tiny minority. Most accept it as reality.

Whether manmade or not, the Earth is warming up. Ice caps are melting. Mountain glaciers may all be gone by as early as 2030 C.E. The Larson Ice Shelves (A and B) in Antarctica are disappearing fast, calving gigantic icebergs off into the ocean (some the size of Delaware), in the process. The Patagonia Ice Fields in South America and the Greenland glaciers are all in full retreat.

Other weird things are happening. Did you know, for example, that in the Alps there is a big problem with the ski lodges? They were built on frozen ground, which when it thaws becomes rubble and sludge that easily slides off the mountains. That soil, for the first time since the last ice age, is now thawing. This means that the lodges could go where no lodges have gone before—down to the bottom of the Alps, and without the aid of skis! Can you say: "Yodel?"

What is not quite so certain is whether this warming phase is a prelude to the onset of another cold period. This new chilly phase could be no worse than the so-called "Little Ice Age" of several centuries ago, or it might be a full-blown ice age, complete with glaciers creeping over continents. Some even fear that we, inadvertently, might be triggering a "snowball earth" effect, where the entire planet freezes over.

This last one is highly debatable. However, the so-called Atlantic Conveyor Belt is a sea current that has shut off in the past. This plunged Europe, North America, and the rest of the world into frigid weather. It may well do it again, and soon, much sooner than most people think. A growing number of scientists are convinced it can take place in less than ten years!

Then there are those that argue that the greenhouse effect is so out of control that it will not allow for any cooling period to take place at all. Earth's climate, they claim, is a runaway juggernaut, and one headed for a Venus-like fate.

What does any of this have to do with writing science fiction, horror, or fantasy? Well, where there is disagreement over such heated questions, there is room for really cool stories. As a writer, you can go with either of the above scenarios, or any combination of both. Even stressing one effect over the other can produce many different possibilities for stories and various slants on them.

"The bitter wind whipped sand in stinging clouds over the frozen desert. It blinded the cold and tired refugees as they struggled southward, away from the encroaching wall of dust-covered glaciers and hordes of cannibals fleeing ahead of them."

Or, "Jamie poled his hastily and ill-constructed raft across the huge and open expanse of water. The sun beat down relentlessly and sweat stung his eyes. He had only the distant tops of the abandoned skyscrapers of El Centro, now just concrete islands awash in that inland sea, to guide him. The marauders were right behind and closing fast."

Get it? There are many great ideas for stories here, science fiction, horror, and fantasy, with settings and plots limited only by one's imagination. People will flee some cities, abandoning them entirely, while other places feel the pressure of influxes of staggering migrations, some of them arriving by violent means. Internationally, balances of power will shift. Nations will crumble, some disappearing completely.

Don't believe me? Well, one historical theory says that Rome, a powerful empire during a five-hundred-year warm spell, fell because of the onset of a much colder time. Hordes of Huns, Goths, Visigoths, and Vandals battered and invaded the frontiers of Rome, seeking a warmer and more prosperous climate. In the process, they committed every sort of gross atrocity. Even to this day, we still refer to something as being "vandalized" if it is intentionally damaged by "vandals." And if this all sounds farfetched, then just remember that during the height of Rome's ascendancy, legionnaires wore sandals (coincidentally?), in the northern reaches of Germany and England, even in winter. One would not do that now, at least, not if one were sane!

Refugee movements will immensely affect your characters' lives. Weather conditions will influence their abilities to feed themselves. Shifts in behavior, as with cannibalism rearing it's ugly head, may happen. Stress on technologies will cause major changes in standards of living. Diseases, once considered strictly tropical, may spread everywhere, and strange new ones may emerge. These are the stuff of great horror stories, as well as science fiction.

Transportation may be difficult or even impossible. How much people get to eat, how much freedom their governments allow (martial law, suspension of constitutions), will all depend on the severity of the climate changes and your characters' responses to it.

Think of innovative ways for your characters to survive. Cities, carved deep into the heart of glaciers, and moving along with them, is one idea. Floating cities, drifting freely on the oceans in once-tropical regions, is another. These would be great scenarios for science fiction, or even fantasy. There could be rogue mobile nuclear power plants, which could crawl around on huge tractor treads and carrying small nomadic towns through frozen wastelands of ice. News mutant species may appear, which would be great for horror stories.

In the case of a full-scale greenhouse effect, mountaintop empires might trade with other such archipelagos across new, vast, and shallow inland seas. Again, these are perfect ideas for science fiction and fantasy stories. Civilizations might grow around the formerly sub-zero Arctic and Antarctic regions, and may be threatened by hosts of barbarians fleeing from the once temperate zones. Vast fleets of ocean-going ships might harbor the remaining survivors of entire nations, now turned to piracy and coastal raiding for survival (see, "Vikings"). Or, how about being holed up in a log cabin, with wolves trying to get at you, but inside, your stuck with several starving cannibals who might eat you as soon as you fall asleep and drop that gun? See what I mean? All of these are ideas for tales in every genre.

There are many such concepts available in just this topic area alone, of how people can survive. And there are equally many possibilities for plots, conflicts, and resolutions. If you need more information on any of these climate phenomena, the Internet is a great place to find it. For instance, just type in "snowball earth" on your search engine, and you will be amazed at the number of hits you get.

Who knows? Someday, some fat and well-oiled tourist on a tropical-like beach in Canada, or some poor starving soul enduring an icy blizzard in Hawaii, may read your story. But, only if it's a good one!

And above all these are ideas from just one of so many available topic areas—write those ideas down! Then when you have writer's block, you have something to fall back upon, in this case, an entire list of ideas. And that's the crux of the matter; it's up to you, yourself, as an author, to expand your own horizons, develop new possibilities for stories. After all, in an infinite universe, there are an infinite number of ideas available, aren't there? Ideas, as "they" say, are where you find them. Just open your eyes, look around you—I had one idea from just watching butterflies. The story that resulted from this was *Dance Of The Butterflies*, and it was published, for good money! So just open yourself to the possibilities. Ideas are all around you.

Now, in the next chapter, we will discuss settings for fantasies, as well as for alternate universe stories, and such. Settings involve more than the average new writer may realize. They are crucial to the story's development, setting the atmosphere of a work, and allowing the characters to play out their parts and plots in a realistic manner. And realism is what it's all about, even for fantasy worlds.

CHAPTER 4

Believable Fantasy Settings For Your Stories

In this chapter, first of several on this subject, we will discuss creating believable settings for your fantasy stories. The following chapters will then deal with science fiction and horror settings, as well, so that all three genres are covered.

Pitfalls Of Writing About The Medieval Ages, Or How Not To End Up As The Village Idiot!

> *"Astride his steed, the Black Knight thundered down the road. He raced passed the old abbey. Its crenellated walls thrust defiantly upward, a holy challenge to the forces of darkness. However, the knight knew that his best hope lay in the hamlet ahead of him. It was there he was to meet the White Wizard. So on he galloped. He passed wattle huts of the outlying and poorest inhabitants. He rode by the quaint stone church with its surprised priest. At last, the knight turned into the main street. The inhabitants scattered like startled pigeons before him. Some ducked inside the bakery. Others fled into the chandler's shop. One panicked citizen, a wealthy merchant, sought shelter with the smithy. The Black Knight reached the Hound and Hunter. It was the hamlet's only inn."*

Right, so that isn't the greatest piece of writing you've ever read. I didn't intend it to be. Rather, it is a bad example, an illustration of things that can go wrong with a story. This happens when writers assume they know more about a given subject than they actually do. Most of us have read enough medieval fantasies to think it is no big deal in using them as settings for our own stories, right? Wrong! Very wrong, as we'll soon see.

Let's start with my bad example. I have my good knight (yes, pun intended, yet again) riding past an abbey situated just outside of the hamlet. In all probability that abbey wasn't there. Moreover, although walled, those walls weren't likely to be crenellated. In addition, I have our friend passing huts, a church with its priest, then down the main street past the usual shops and smithy until he reaches the local inn. Wrong, wrong, and wrong again. A village, by historical definition, had at least six houses. A hamlet had less. Therefore, there wouldn't be any outlying wattle hovels. There would barely be any houses at all. In addition, there was no main street. If anything, it was a wide spot in the road and that was about it. Four or five homes clustered near each other and nothing else, not even a church. You see, another historical definition of a hamlet was that it didn't have a church. Maybe it was lucky enough to have a small chapel, but that chapel would not have had a resident priest, surprised or otherwise.

We also have to dispense with my bakery and blacksmith. Oh, and forget the wealthy merchant. He wouldn't have lived in such a hole-in-the-wall place. Lose the inn as well. Unless it's on a well-traveled highway, there wouldn't have been enough customers to keep it going. Finally, the chandler has to go, too. You see, usually there were no businesses at all in a hamlet. One other thing; watch out for young thieves running over rooftops and hiding behind chimney pots, as in Raymond E. Feist's, *Riftwar Saga* novels. That's right—no chimneys! They didn't appear until the late Thirteenth Century and then only for the very rich to enjoy. Earlier, even castles suffered along without them.

You see, a hamlet was tiny. Usually, people situated them where several farmers' adjacent properties met or came together. That was it; not much of anything else, except perhaps, a lot of inbreeding and relations that were far too close for legal comfort, but I digress.

Now let's be fair here; obviously nobody is going to raise a hue and cry (I've always wanted to use that phrase) or kick you out of the fantasy genre as being a bad author just because you happen to call a small village a hamlet, or vice versa. For an otherwise well-written and accurate novel, the occasional slip-up will usually go unnoticed by the reader, or they simply won't care if the do notice it. However, tossing all sorts of anachronisms into a story is a much bigger issue. This causes major problems with the realism of your tale. You've just read the hash I made of that hamlet in my example. Get the point? Describing a true medieval hamlet, village, town, or city isn't nearly as easy as one would imagine, but it is important to do it right.

Just how imperative is it? Well, that depends on whether you are writing a fantasy that is meant more as a work of historical fiction (that feeling of gritty reality we all love), or whether you are creating your own personal universe, as a setting for your particular work. If it's a fantasy or alternate history set in our world, it's an absolute must to get it as historically correct as possible, because readers know their stuff! Many of them often read stories about the Middle Ages because they like and want to learn more about that period. It's why I read Michael Crighton's, *Timeline,* for instance. (However, the less said about that particular novel here, the better.)

With a fantasy universe, anachronisms are not such a looming issue. In any author's personal creation, houses for instance, could have chimneys. After all, it's their universe. They can do what they want with it. Hard to argue with that logic, isn't it? Besides which, it just isn't a terrible offense to make the occasional anachronistic mistake. Shakespeare even did it (often). Coincidentally, one involved chimney tops. In his play, *Julius Caesar*, he spoke of them as being in ancient Rome. Wrong! None existed at that time. He also had clocks, church bells, and other things there as well. Wrong again! They were yet to be invented.

Still, there is one important caveat that you, as an author, should always remember. Your readers, as I've said, will forgive you the odd little mistake (oh, those chimneys), and overlook slightly misused words (village-versus-hamlet), but they aren't stupid. Too glaring a mistake or just too many mistakes in accuracy and people (editors?) will notice. Trust me; that will be to the detriment of your story and possibly your budding career as well.

Don't just take my word for it. Your readers are the final and most powerful judges. As an example, an independent reader and reviewer of David Edding's historical fantasy, *Domes of Fire*, referred to it as having "teeth grinding anachronisms," specifically such as "...cookie and mom...." He felt that the author had been just plain "lazy."

Now that's not a good review when you're trying to sell books, is it? Of course, David has written many excellent stories and the rare clinker will not destroy him. Besides, his descriptions of castles and fortresses were highly accurate with their outer and inner wards, keeps, and crenellated walls. Still, for new authors, such types of reviews may have more dire consequences. (Try to remember those budding careers! You don't want them nipped in the bud.)

With real-world historical fantasies or science fiction, it is essential to be accurate. Another reviewer, Alex Ford, of Patrick Tilley's book, *Fade Out*, had this to say about it:

"I've only read one third so far but am already annoyed by the anachronisms thrown up.... For example, when written the book obviously dealt with a President who fought in the Pacific theatre during WWII." [But] "...the introduction to the President's military background states that he finished his aviation training just as the Vietnam War ended."

That would make an ace World War II pilot of the early Nineteen-Forties not completing his necessary flight training for it until the mid Nineteen-Seventies, some thirty odd years after World War II ended. That's not a minor mistake, but rather one that interfered with the reader's willing suspension of disbelief, and even worse, in this case, it "annoyed" the reader. (Major rule: Never annoy your readers!) Yet, despite this gaffe, Mr. Tilley did give concise and detailed descriptions of the various types of fighter planes used, their maneuverability, and how battles actually occurred. Therefore, on many subjects, his research was top-notch, but apparently not all. And that mistake was enough to garner him a bad review.

Another example, one that personally bothered me a lot, was the "glaring anachronisms" as one critic put it, in the film, **Pirates of the Caribbean**. The writers for that film set major portions of the story in Port Royal, Jamaica. Unfortunately, Port Royal had disappeared under the sea in a disastrous quake long before the events of this story ever took place. Yes, I know it was successful and a movie, but it was also a piece of historical fantasy set in the real world; it was wrong and somebody wrote it that way. I noticed. People watching the film noticed (e.g., "glaring anachronisms"). Moreover, books and unlike cinema, rely solely upon their individual merit. Johnny Depp won't magically appear to save a badly researched novel. Get it?

Therefore, I repeat, this much remains true regardless of whether it's a factually based fantasy done in our own Middle Ages, or one created in another universe—getting it right is always important, very important. And just as a side note to this, even with regard to the mighty Shakespeare and his anachronisms, I'd like to point out that essays often discuss them and sometimes not in a good way. Get it again? Nobody's immune to destructive criticism, although some can weather it better than others can.

Anachronistic problems aside, now we know the differences between a village and a hamlet. Right? (You do, don't you?) However, do you know the differences between a village and a town, a town and a borough, or a borough and a city? Which ones had marketplaces? What were they really like and what are authors' usual mistakes in portraying them?

Well first, let's remember the period we're talking about and what it was like. *Medium Aevum* (Latin), or the Middle Ages, refers to a period that loosely covers the time from the fall of the Roman Empire (476 C.E.) to the rise of the Renaissance. That's a long time and authors forget that many changes occurred during it. So costuming, shoes, etc., are important to research. You don't want your hero-prince dressed in Thirteenth Century clothing, but sporting Ninth Century shoes. How déclassé; people would talk and not in a good way!

Many famous authors, such as Mary Stewart of the *Crystal Cave*, make these kinds of mistakes, including most who write about King Arthur. You see, in the late Fifth Century, warriors *rarely* wore metal armor in England or Europe, but rather specially toughened leather. British male royalty and nobility still wore their hair in the Roman fashion—short—not the long streaming warrior locks we now visualize them having. After all, Romances had only left just a few years before and fashions simply hadn't changed that quickly. In all likelihood, if King Arthur existed then, and contrary to most authors' descriptions of him, he was probably not and neither were his knights, dressed in shining armor. They might have had breast plates or chain mail, but again, probably not full suits of shining armor. Moreover, they probably wore their hair quite short. (Sort of ruins the image of it all, doesn't it?)

During the medieval period, the vast majority of people lived the manor lifestyle. There would be the local lord with his castle, a church or chapel, farmland, and a village or hamlet. Towns were rare and cities much more so. The manor lifestyle had an agrarian-based economy with only the occasional stranger in the form of a peddler, troubadour, or pilgrim intruding into the daily lives of its people.

As a writer, you should remember this. To be realistic, your characters in such a setting should be at least a little xenophobic, that is suspicious of newcomers, although probably still eager for news of the outside world, as well. I know, it's contradictory, but then people often are. However, it does make for creating some fun characters.

Some villages grew to become towns and then cities, while some towns simply grew around a convenient market place where people from different villages met (hence, the English reference to "market towns"). The difference between a town and a large village is then, of necessity, a little vague. Still, and unlike hamlets, most scholars define them as having switched to a merchant and market-based economy from an agrarian one. Therefore, whether you have a large village or a small town, it should have merchants and marketplaces where people barter, sell, and exchange goods. And, it would definitely have a church instead of just a chapel with a part-time priest.

Authors often stumble over these facts. I've read numerous stories where good-sized villages, even towns and cities, were in the middle of nowhere and with no visible means of support. Of course, this means no trade and so presumably no merchants, and no market place. Whoops! Another one of David Eddings' novels of the *Belgariad* series had a big village located amidst swamps or "fens." Yet oddly enough, the population lived with many comforts. Just how did they manage to come by these things? Was it by living off frogs' legs and using dried mud balls to trade for these goods? Was their annual festival fen frolicking? What did they burn for fuel on those damp winter nights—swamp gas? You see, it's just not a very believable setting. That village needed a rational source of income. It needed a valid reason for being wherever it was, and the size it was. I'll tell you what it really needed—a new location! However, David was very realistic at describing other things, such as the physical discomfort of wearing armor. He was right. It was prone to rusting, rubbing, itching, and smelling.

Towns called boroughs were different from other towns and villages in that they were self-governing; made independent of their lords by paying an annual tax to them. They did this because many villages were actually the property of their local lord and what he said was law. The way to get around that was to become a borough. The word borough derives from the Old English word, *burh*. It referred originally to simple fortified places, but later came to include larger population centers with defenses, usually consisting of earthworks and/or walls. So, remember to wall or barricade that borough you create. Oh, and the word *town* was a description only used in England. Nobody on the European continent made such a distinction. If your setting is, say, in Germany, Denmark, France, or some other continental place, it might be wiser to avoid calling anything a town.

Cities of the Middle Ages were not like the cities of today. Ours are melting pots with fluid and interchanging classes of society. This wasn't the case then. We're talking about a time of rigid class and economic structure—incredibly so. In those days, people didn't leave the farms for a better life in the city, because there was virtually no upward mobility in either place—once a peasant, always a peasant, almost without exception. Authors who have their serf hero trooping off to strike it rich in medieval London are making a cardinal error. It just wouldn't have happened unless, of course, the serf intended to become a criminal, because just leaving his land was a crime. He belonged to, for all practical purposes, the noble who owned that land.

Merchants may get wealthy, but they answered to their betters just as surely as their servants had to answer to them. Nobility, not pleased with the wealth of merchants and guilds, passed sumptuary laws. These laws forbade non-nobles from wearing certain types of clothing, shoes, and jewelry that were too reminiscent of the nobles own costumes. In Chaucer's time, for instance, nobility forbade merchants to wear jewelry made of silver, so they wore silver knives and daggers instead, thus dodging those laws. (Don't you just hate social climbers? The nobles apparently did.)

The point here is that there are more than just physical anachronisms. There are the social or philosophical ones as well. Writers often erroneously subscribe to their characters modern-day viewpoints and belief systems that didn't exist during the Middle Ages in villages or cities. Freedom of expression, equal rights, feminism, or freedom of religion just weren't factors in everyday life then.

Guilds, as in villages and towns, also existed in cities. They were often powerful, wealthy, and exercised considerable political force in later years, but not so much during the early Middle Ages. Their focus was hanging onto their particular piece of a city's monopolized commercial pie. Loopholes in these monopolies were few, but some existed. A loophole created restaurants. The different guilds controlled all types of food making, from bakeries to butchers. Later, an enterprising merchant in France, one, A. Boulanger, opened a place in Paris that sold soup. Guilds considered soups less as food and more as health restoratives, or "restaurants" in French, so they didn't bother to control it. Thus, restaurants came into being. (Fascinating stuff, isn't it? Don't answer that...) Again, although such loopholes were rare, there were some. This fact may be of use in writing your fantasy. It's one way your characters could get around the strict restrictions of that society.

Cities of the Middle Ages often had universities and definitely cathedrals, along with all the support staff, servants, and materials such institutions entailed. In fact, this was one of the main definitions of a city; it had a cathedral versus a church for a town or village, and a chapel or nothing for a hamlet.

Many authors forget or downplay the power the Church wielded in cities of the Middle Ages. David Eddings, luckily, did not fall into this trap. In his *Domes of Fire*, he had his heroes coming from a rigidly religious, medieval, and theocratic state. He was very detailed about its character, nature, and iron-gripping power. It did not tolerate heresy. This is an excellent real-life portrayal.

However, I've read other stories where various authors never mention any church at all, let alone a cathedral, as being in their metropolis. Furthermore, they often have their bigwigs deciding important matters without any clergymen involved. This is a glaring error. No major decisions about a city, including its defenses, economics, or anything else, ever happened without the presence or potent influence of a priest, bishop, archbishop, or cardinal. Even much later, the enormous power of Cardinal Richelieu under King Louis of France is legendary.

Stories that ignore the potent role of the Church then, do not seem very realistic. Raymond E. Feist, in his *Riftwar Saga* had cathedrals, but he really didn't dwell enough on the power and influence of the church, in my opinion. His religions came across more as cult followings of various gods, rather than powerful state monotheisms. That creates a conundrum, because small cults worshipping obscure gods, but creating such vast expensive edifices as cathedrals would have been highly problematical. Oh, and he had chimney tops, too! (Can't seem to get away from those, can we?)

Mr. Feist was excellent, however, at portraying most other aspects of medieval city life. His cities had richness to them when it came to detailing the architecture of such cathedrals (flying buttresses, naves, stone columns, etc.), the everyday life of the inhabitants, dress, and economics. Just remember though, that authors miss a real opportunity to add depth and dimension to their work when they fail to portray powerful churches as a big part of that life. After all, there's nothing like an evil prelate to give a story a lively interest!

Cities often had ports, were major hubs of trade and commerce, and unlike villages, they often constituted the political centers of power. Cities could result from the growing together of towns or boroughs that were located near each other, and so traded closely with each other. The ancients founded some cities deliberately. The Romans built Londinium, now modern London, in just this way. Constantinople, now modern-day Istanbul, is another example of this. So again, location is important, as any real estate agent will tell you. Site your towns and cities where there is a reason for them to be, such as at the crossroads of major trade routes, along a navigable river, or near a deepwater harbor.

Why worry about these distinctions between hamlets, villages, towns, and cities? Why be so thorough and careful about what's in them and where they're located? The answer is simple; again, it's willing suspension of disbelief. If your readers aren't buying your setting, they cannot and will not suspend their disbelief in your story. To put it another way; they'll think your work is garbage! Worse, so will those infamously fussy editors to whom you submit your fantasy. Again, this is not to say that some fudging isn't okay. Small village or big hamlet; who really cares? Just don't go too far with it.

Less important, but still a factor, is trying to avoid the more common writers' pitfalls. For example, don't have the innkeeper serving his customers their food at a table and the characters then using forks to eat it. In reality, people brought their own boards upon which the innkeeper placed their food (hence the term "bread and board"). They used only a knife and/or a spoon. Forks were an invention of the Italians during the later

Renaissance Period. ("Sporks" came much later and only after the invention of plastic.) Oh, and villagers and townsfolk really did love to gossip. However, there were no local coffee houses—no coffee, or tea for that matter, so the local church was also the local gossip centre along with inns.

To have a good fantasy or alternate-reality science fiction story set in our medieval period, or the author's own universe, is to have one that seems realistic. Therefore, you as the author should know your subject. Research it. I'd wager that most fantasy authors aren't even aware that there are technical differences between hamlets or villages, or that the classification of communities such as villages or cities involved the type of church they had.

Know your subject, because only in a well thought-out world can characters truly flourish, be three-dimensional people to the reader, and be a place where a good plot about them can unfold. Whether you use a city, town, borough, village, or hamlet, try to portray it as a place where real people lived, worked, and sometimes played. Beware! If you don't take care in your writing to do this, to strive for accuracy and realism, then you may end up not as a successful writer, but rather as the village idiot. Luckily, I think hamlets were too small even to have those…

Now, how about settings purely designed for science fiction stories? Those can be even tougher, as we'll see in this next chapter.

CHAPTER 5

Custom Planets And Realistic Fantasy/Horror Worlds

> *"You can do it, my boy. The plane is trustworthy and I have faith in you." The old pilot pointed his gnarled arthritic finger at their world's twin planet, Ourobouros. It loomed on the horizon, a great dull-red hemisphere with swirling dirty bands of gray. It dominated their night sky.*
>
> *"At midpoint, the air thins to almost nothing," the ancient pilot said. "You will have to switch from the propellers over to the chemical rockets. Don't use them too long. You will need them to get back. Once you are fully into the air of Ourobouros, you can turn on the gasoline engines again. This trip would not be possible if our two planets weren't so close as to share each other's atmospheres. Think of it, Arkon. You will be the first to fly a plane to our neighboring planet. You will be our world's greatest hero!"*

No, he won't. It is most unlikely that Arkon and his people could have existed in the first place, let alone being able to fly standard airplanes, even with rocket assistance, to a neighboring planet. Even his world's very survival is highly unlikely. Bummer, isn't it?

Edgar Rice Burroughs was one of the first authors to use such types of scenarios. In fact, he wrote a novel based on that very idea. And as always when one is successful, there were a lot of copycat writers who wrote stories that followed his original premise. To be fair, such premises seemed reasonable enough back then. After all, the Earth and Moon form what some would consider a double-planet system, so there was a real and close example of such a thing being possible, or so the average science fiction reader thought at the time. Give both planets atmospheres and there might be air all the way between them. That's a cool premise. And readers flocked to buy books based upon such ideas and themes.

It wasn't that the average reader was less skeptical back then or stupid, but most of them were just not well versed in the hard sciences of today. They were more innocent and naïve. Remember, many people, even in the fifties, sixties, and seventies, thought that rockets were "pushed" into space by their own exhaust rather than "reacting" to it. Sadly, even now, some still think this. This is so, despite the fact that Newtown's Third Law of Motion has been known and been around since the early 1700's. Oh, well! But the point is, if you as a reader didn't know something was impossible then you could go ahead and willingly suspend your disbelief. With such a naive public, writers could get away with just about anything they wished. And they did!

But times have changed and now readers are a much savvier and therefore vicious lot. (For that matter, so are editors, but then, I think *they* were always that way.) So if we writers tried such scenarios now, we would have an angry mob of insulted readers after us. And there is nothing worse than an angry mob. Just ask Frankenstein. Like it or not, readers have come a long way in knowing about science, knowing what's possible, and more importantly, what is not. Genres have hardened. For example, most people don't like it when pure fantasy mixes with science fiction. Readers who enjoy science fiction want it to sound plausible and possible, or they just aren't interested. I know. I'm one of them.

And Arkon's world isn't—possible, I mean. At least, not the way I have it described. You see, natural laws make the premise of my story impractical. The Roche limit forbids two planets of similar composition existing so close together. 2.5 times the radius of the larger of the two bodies is as close as they can get before they would tear each other apart through mutual tidal gravitational forces. Even if (and a very small "if") for some reason they did not at first, the gravitational friction would slow down their orbits to the point where one of them would soon spiral into a rather spectacular disintegration with the other. In other words, to exist, they'd have to be quite a ways apart and their atmospheres would not intermingle in any meaningful way. After all the average distance from the Moon to the Earth is less than 250,000 miles and none of Earth's air makes it there (not counting that belonging to visiting astronauts).

What's that you say? In your story, Arkon lived on his world before its destruction happened? Okay, but still his people would have faced horrific tides, constant and tremendous earthquakes, and let's not even mention the problems they would have with volcanoes! (Yeah, I know—I just mentioned them.) And what about days and nights? Gravitational tidal forces would have forced the planets to have only one of their faces forever turned toward the other, circling each other in locked step, as our poor Moon does with Earth. That means days and nights would be similar or longer than our own Moon's month-long day. It would get unbelievably hot during those long daytimes and bitterly cold during the nights. Storms would be ferocious; perhaps seas might even migrate as they repeatedly evaporated and froze around the planet. At the very least, you'd have some darn big ice caps and a very narrow belt of livable area. Try living on that kind of a world and evolve a modern civilization! Evolution itself would have a very tough time, indeed. But if you could work it out, it would make for a great setting for a story, wouldn't it?

Get the point? If you want to call your story science fiction or science fiction horror, then you have to keep in mind the basic laws of our universe. Even the horror movie, Pitch Black, was very careful about this, to keep the moviegoer's willing suspension of disbelief, at least, while watching the movie. Actually, that goes just as much for fantasies, too. There must be a very set rules for the use of magic, any sort of magic, or the stories just aren't believable. So, as annoying as it is to have to remember those basic natural or unnatural laws, it is necessary if you want to write a credible story regardless of genre, one that is based on a convincing premise, and most importantly, one that will placate those vicious readers out there. A fiction writer's lot is not an easy one, is it?

So, how do we make up a planet, solar system, or fantasy world that fulfills our particular requirements, one that fits the premise of our story? Well, there are three major ways of approaching it. The first one is simply to make up a solar system that is similar to our own, plus or minus a few planets and conditions. Then give it some largely cosmetic changes to accommodate our story's settings. Do you want your colony or fantasy planet to be a little colder than Earth? Move it slightly farther away from its sun. Do you want it to be more desert-like? Move it a little closer or take away some of its water. Alternatively, give it more or less greenhouse gasses as needed to produce the same effects, or even use combinations of these factors to achieve the desired results.

You see, this method uses our known worlds (Earth, Mars, Jupiter, etc.) as templates, and reworks them a little to fit your specific needs. Then you can people them with whatever you want, within reason. Raymond Feist and David Eddings both did this for their fantasy worlds. This way your world merely requires slight alterations in what we already know are real and workable planets. So it's the quickest and easiest way to go. (And we aren't faced with those irritating torch-wielding mobs shouting "no willing suspension of disbelief!").

The second method is to use current astronomical data from various sources, such as the Internet, **Science Magazine, Analog, Scientific American, Discover**, and others. From these, you can glean the information of what other star systems are factually supposed to be like. You can then use this knowledge to construct realistic settings in the real universe for your story. Although an accurate and hard science way to go, it is a time-consuming and laborious one. And it has limitations. Your planets must adhere closely to reality. That can be tough to do. For instance, what would the orbital pattern of a world be that circled a sun that in turn orbited a black hole? What would the planet's seasons be like? How long and how extreme would they be? Don't ask me, because I don't know either. But I'll bet some of your readers would. They always seem to and they're the ones that will write those nasty letters to your editors. If you don't believe me, then try checking out the letters section of *Analog*.

And this means you run the risk of making your work irrelevant, whether science fiction, fantasy, or horror. After all, the horror movie, **Pitch Black**, relied extensively on its planetary setting. The *John Carter of Mars* series by Edgar Rice Burroughs was a great classic set of tales, but nobody today would believe they were remotely possible, because everyone knows what Mars is really like now—sterile, barren, and little atmosphere (and the wrong kind), and very cold! *John Carter*, those marvelous novels, are now reduced to being just "quaint" to most present-day readers. If you're not careful, your work could end up that way before it is even published; that is, if it ever gets published with such type settings. Remember those editors! They're a picky lot. Same holds true for fantasy settings. Have a poorly constructed world/universe for your story, and you've probably already lost your readers before you've even started.

The third way is to hire a scientist to create worlds for you. Oh yes, some actually do that, but for a price, of course. (You might get them cheaper from a graduate student, but the quality might not be as good—no reputations to destroy yet, so no big worry for them if they get it wrong for you.) But it is true that some scientists will build planets from the ground up, so to speak, that suit your needs, and ones that are scientifically accurate (for the most part). Or if you're short on cash and you happen to have a good basic knowledge of sciences, then you can use this knowledge to construct your worlds using this same technique.

This last one is tricky. The science can be difficult and so mistakes are easy to make. You see, no matter how good your knowledge is; it's what you don't know that can be the problem. As an example, say you want an earthlike world, but one without a sizeable and/or nearby moon like our own. No problem, right? Well, your planet would wobble wildly on its axis, even possibly flopping over on its "sides" at times. This would make for extreme weather and therefore, life, very difficult if not impossible on it. Many scientists believe that complex life simply couldn't evolve on a world of such extreme conditions. In others, words, it takes a moon, or some other stabilizing force to calm things down.

All right then, let's now make this even easier. How about just having an earthlike world that circles a gas giant, as in the series of stories in **Asimov's Science Fiction Magazine** set on the planet *Coyote*? Again, there would be problems. The surfaces of planets closely circling such huge worlds could be barren, sterilized by hard radiation, as with the types that Jupiter emits. Tidal forces would do nasty things to the smaller planet's crust on a more than regular basis (there go those darn high tides, earthquakes, and volcanoes again!). And so the problems go; planets circling around hot blue stars would have a tough time with the increased energy and radiation outputs of those suns. Tiny worlds cannot keep their atmospheres long enough to develop advanced life (see, the Moon, and/or Mars). Again, you see, it's what you don't know that can hurt you. Make big changes and you make big problems, some unforeseen by you as a writer, but noticed by that persnickety and sneaky little reader, or that dastardly editor.

But don't despair. With a little finagling, one can get around many of these problems. The author of the planet *Coyote* stories did. And you can, too. For example, if radiation from a gas giant is the trouble, use a stronger and more protective magnetic field to shield your world, or move it farther away from its Jovian parent. Do you want a world the size of Earth but with a stronger gravity? Just give the world's composition a higher ratio of dense materials versus lighter ones. For a lighter gravity, just reverse that ratio. Want a terrestrial world but with a green-colored atmosphere? Well, just come up with some type of tiny chlorophyll-carrying plants that float in abundance in the air (maybe hydrogen or helium filled). It worked for the novel, *After Worlds Collide*. That blue star too hot for you? Move your planet farther away from it.

The important thing here is to be reasonable about what you do. Keep in mind that you can't go too far or the planet simply wouldn't be practical. For example, making the gravity of an earthlike-sized world too light (so your humans can fly with wings), would make life as we know it probably impossible. So as with most things, be moderate in your changes, because extreme changes often call for extreme and lengthy explanations. Those are annoying to the reader. There's nothing worse than a three-page info dump on how a starship drive works, for instance.

And readers aren't really as vicious as I've claimed (I think). Most of them are willing to overlook much that might seem slightly odd or wrong with the worlds you build, as long as you give them plausible-sounding explanations. Or as with fantasy settings; keep them consistent! Rules are rules, even in the realm of magic. Horror story settings tend to more like hard science fiction ones. They have to be very believable in the practical sort of way, or at least internally consistent within themselves. But keep explanations for things just a little vague. Don't go into too many aspects of it. Remember, readers can't nitpick over details that aren't there, and what's more, you don't want to fall into the "info dump" problem by overdoing your explanations.

The first method I mentioned above, that of making minor changes to planets of our known solar system is probably your best bet. And it can make for some interesting worlds, too, because little changes add up to big cosmetic differences. To prove my point, let's play with that idea.

Let's take our Earth and make some relatively small alterations to it. We won't do anything too big, because we don't know what all the consequences and ramifications of doing that might entail (although our readers always seem to). And if we get minor things wrong, the average reader won't notice it or they'll just probably overlook it if they do. Let's include some of the things I've already mentioned just to make it even easier.

Okay, what do we do first? Well for starters, let's change our new world's continents to a vast number of islands scattered in archipelagoes. We'll also move the planet somewhat farther (a little) out from its sun. We'll make the sun just a little older and orange while we're at it. Now, we'll make our planet a bit smaller and slightly reduce its denser materials versus its lighter ones. Also, we'll shrink the moon by about a fifth, and add two much tinier ones. See, small changes, but a considerable number of them.

What do we now have? Well, it would be a world with a tiny orange sun in the sky during the day, and a trio of moons, which sometimes would all appear in the night sky at the same time, and sometimes not. It would be a cold place overall, perhaps locked in the grip of a permanent ice age, or even a snowball-earth phase. At the very least, it should have very sizeable ice caps and/or even partially frozen seas in its Arctic and Antarctic regions. This could be ameliorated some by high greenhouse gas content in its atmosphere (perhaps from an inordinate number of volcanoes). Gravity would be noticeably lighter. Heavy elements would be harder to find and in short supply for intelligent species to find, and use in their civilizations. Cultures there might be metal starved and have to use creative substitutes. I'm reminded of the fantasy *Rift-War Sagas*, in this regard, where the invaders came from such a world, and so used ceramics, hardened paper products, etc., and such other substitutes in their weapons and armor. Also, there should be large arid areas on my world, because with so much of the water locked in ice, there wouldn't be a lot of moisture left in the air for good precipitation. Frigid temperate zone deserts might be the result.

Your aliens would have to be a seafaring and/or ice-trudging race (or both), one that mainly inhabits and girdles the planet's equatorial belt, since that would be the kindest area, climatologically speaking. And how would evolution proceed on so many isolated islands? Would there be a lot of diversity? Would you have more than one sentient race?

You see? It would be a very alien world and all we did was make some minor changes to it from our own Earth. Again, although there might be things wrong with our scenario, they don't leap out at one, and thus our setting seems plausible to the average reader, and hopefully, the average editor, too. So again, this method for a writer (who doesn't also happen to be a scientist), might be the best choice. Just remember, the setting doesn't have to be perfect, just plausible, and reasonable. And as with science fiction settings, horror and fantasy ones must also be this same way, or at least, they should be internally self-consistent. To break your own rules for such a world, you'd better have a darn good reason, one that will hold up with the readers.

And have hope, because if none of these methods works for you and all else fails, you can just do what I do. That is, you can invoke some powerful (alien?) super science to explain how your solar system or planets can exist, or be so strange. In the case of fantasy, it can be the "gods'" doing. With horror, maybe the nameless horror is, itself, the cause? Hey, why not? If it works for all the current big-named authors (who shall remain nameless), it's good enough for us, right? But do keep in mind that you (1) must create a believable setting [preferably using one of the methods above], (2) keep your settings internally self-consistent, whether science fiction, fantasy, or horror, and if you don't, have (3) a darn good reason why your are not following your own settings' rules and limitations.

Now that we have the basic idea of what's involved in settings, we need to know a little about variations on them. For instance, how do we create an entire "universe" for our science fiction, fantasy, or horror story? Where else can we look for setting? What's more, once having created that universe, how do we create a specific atmosphere, a certain feel we want to give our stories? Although absolutely necessary for all genres of stories, atmosphere is particularly necessary in works of horror, and only marginally less so in science fiction and fantasy. In fact, some authors and readers would say atmosphere is everything! In the following chapters, we will discuss how to find more variations on finding settings for our stories, how to create "universes" for them, and to develop a specific atmosphere for our work.

CHAPTER 6

Creating Universes—Real Or Imagined. Believe In Magic?

> *"BY a route obscure and lonely,*
>
> *Haunted by ill angels only,*
>
> *Where an Eidolon, named NIGHT,*
>
> *On a black throne reigns upright,*
>
> *I have reached these lands but newly*
>
> *From an ultimate dim Thule*
>
> *From a wild weird clime that lieth, sublime,*
>
> *Out of SPACE - out of TIME."*

...Excerpt from *Dreamland*, by Edgar Allen Poe

There's no one like good old Edgar for setting a mood, is there? More importantly, this verse from *Dreamland* says concisely and precisely (couldn't pass that rhyme up) what I'm about to take a thousand words to do. Okay, so he's a better writer than I am. That's why I'm quoting him! In addition, the fact that he wrote this stuff in the Nineteenth Century absolutely amazes (dare I say, flabbergasts?) me. He creates not just a universe, but fills it with mood and feeling as well; as writers, we must strive to do the same.

We, like Poe, want to create different universes for the settings of our various stories. First, though, we should consider what constitutes a universe. Webster's Dictionary defines it as:

"...the whole body of things and phenomena observed or postulated: cosmos... a systematic whole held to arise by and persist through the direct intervention of divine power... (1): the entire celestial cosmos... 2: a distinct field or province of thought or reality that forms a closed system...."

Okay, so that's a real mouthful, but let's break it down and discuss the parts pertinent to science fiction, horror, and fantasy writers. For hard science fiction writers, we can think of a universe as being something like our own cosmos. That is, physically real; complete with planets, stars, and galaxies. Whether or not some deity divinely created, or inspired it, is usually not important for hard sci-fi writers. They just don't deal with that part of things, unlike fantasy writers who often do. Many authors place their stories in our own particular universe, or a reality so similar, as to be indiscernible from it. I think of it as taking the easy road—that is, deal with what you (sort of) know. Many writers, but not all, do this. Some take our universe and change the natural laws to create something more amenable to their needs. You must do this carefully if you do. Remember the chapter on creating your own worlds, having to abide by the laws of physics and such? Well, it's even harder when you tamper with those physics. The important thing if you do this is to be internally self-consistent within that universe. However something normally works there, is how it should always work, unless you come up with a convincing explanation as to why not. This same holds true for fantasy writers.

Deviate too far from our own reality and your universe falls under the second Webster's definition. Fantasy writers do this to make magic (Magick?) work. They create a reality that forms its own internally consistent and closed system. These fabricated universes, often much like ours in most respects, also allow magical laws to work. This means creatures and beings can exist that just couldn't in our own cosmos.

Now, what is the main criterion in such a closed system, whether be it a magical universe or one with just different physical laws from our own?

Again, **CONSISTENCY!**

I've said it before and I'm saying it again. Whatever attributes you subscribe to your particular universe, they must be internally self-consistent. You can't, as the creator of that universe, make basic laws—magical, scientific, or otherwise, and then proceed to break them whenever you choose, willy-nilly. That's a big no-no! If you do, the story and plot will break down; the characters will not have cohesion. So carefully formulate and then write down your own "universal" laws. Make certain that everyone and every thing in your story sticks to them.

Translation: Whatever your beings, plots, and settings; they must proceed under usually unbreakable rules. If not, then you'd better have a "realistic" explanation for your readers as to why not. This bears repeating, because it's just so important when creating such universes/settings for your stories.

For authors who want to stick to the known universe (so to speak), and still get a little outlandish—do not despair. Science of late has come up with some interesting notions. For instance, one theory states that if our universe is truly infinite as scientists usually define it, then just using normal laws of physics and probability, means that given enough time and chance, just about everything that can happen will happen. That means there could be any number of other "Earths" created out there, somewhere far away in the sky, where we have come into being, but with only minor changes to our lives and ourselves, while others are widely disparate. I know, it sounds like parallel universes, and they are, sort of, but they all take place somewhere within our own real and infinite universe. Cool, huh?

Speaking of parallel universes (we were, weren't we?); many scientists are beginning to accept the multiverse theory with infinite parallel "stacked" universes as being a model for our true reality. This quote from the *New Scientist Guide* regarding David Deutsch, University of Oxford, England, states:

"The evidence for the multiverse, according to Deutsch, is equally overwhelming. "Admittedly, it's indirect," he says. "But then, we can detect pterodactyls and quarks only indirectly too. The evidence that other universes exist is at least as strong as the evidence for pterodactyls or quarks."

The funny part about this multiverse controversy is that scientists don't seem to be arguing so much about whether or not there is such a thing, but rather specifically, what exact form it takes, and how it works.

What does all this mean? Well, it signifies that you as a writer can use our "real" universe, parallel ones, or ones constructed by yourself for your own purposes with their own laws of physics or magic, and that you have a heck of a lot of latitude in doing it without suspending readers' disbelief. Isn't that great? Just remember, you may bend a reader's willing suspension of disbelief, but do not break it!

There is one last thing to remember, however. No matter what universe you make, you must remember to give it life, tone, and mood. As with Edgar Allen Poe, breathe a strangeness and freshness into it. Make it "an ultimate dim Thule" or "a wild weird clime that lieth" (lieth??), "sublime," or "Out of SPACE - out of TIME." If you can do that, then you will have achieved the truly remarkable. Probably, being published and becoming famous will then be unavoidable for you. Now, if I could just figure out how to do that for me...in any case, now let's discuss settings just a bit more, before dealing with atmosphere for your book.

CHAPTER 7

Settings For Writers Who Just Want To Stay At Home!

The wormhole was open at last. Kevin, clad in the very latest protective environmental suit, stepped through it.

SNAP!

He stood on the surface of a strange world. A monstrous gibbous moon hung just above the eastern horizon. It dominated the black-reddish sky. Stars could not compete with its brilliance. His readouts showed a complete lack of oxygen and deadly levels of carbon dioxide. There seemed to be no life anywhere and it was hot, very hot. Air pressure was incredibly high, and only Kevin's suit saved him from being crushed. He felt a shudder. Earthquake! Where he stood, the ground pitched and rolled beneath him and then lifted high. Boulders clattered and tumbled. Rocks rolled and crashed. An alarm sounded. Kevin glanced at his altimeter. He, and the darkling plain with him, had just risen almost a kilometer high!

Just then, a strange dark wall appeared on the horizon. He heard an incredibly loud rumble. Kevin realized, belatedly, the wall was a giant wave of black water rushing toward him. It must be a thousand meters high! Just as he stepped through the wormhole again, it occurred to him that the moon of this world hadn't been as large as he'd first thought, but just very close to the planet, instead, and so creating the tremendous tides.

SNAP!

He stood on the edge of a slumping cliff. Below him, receding into the distance was an ancient seabed, an endless expanse of vitreous, ochre-and-yellow sand dunes. They looked like waves of frozen Venetian glass. There was almost no atmosphere at all on this world. Unfamiliar stars glittered brittle and hard in the night sky.

Then, a startling line of crimson appeared across two-thirds of the horizon. A vermillion sliver peeped above the lines of dunes there. The sliver grew into a monstrous crescent of ruby sun, great spots clearly visible on its roiling, heaving, and seething surface. His readouts showed the heat and radiation levels soaring as the scarlet sun rose.

In the distance, he could see the dunes glisten sanguinely, looking red-wet, as they began to melt once again with the heat of a new-born day, one born from hell. He waited no longer. He would die here if he didn't leave. Without hesitation, he stepped through the wormhole once more.

SNAP!

Okay, I think we must all have the point by now. Barring just a touch of literary license (more or less—probably more), these scenes could well have been Earth at one time or another, and probably actually were to some degree. The first scene was meant to be from early Earth not long after the oceans had formed. The last one was our planet in the far future, before our dying red sun engulfed it. Of course, there may have been no sunrise, because the Earth might have just one face eternally locked toward the sun by then. So this was just a touch of literary license here, if you will.

You see, we think of our planet as being static in its environment and only undergoing changes slowly, over vast amounts of time. But we forget just how different the Earth was at various stages of its existence. Yes, we all know about the dinosaurs and the ice ages. We know how different things must have been then, but I don't believe most of us truly comprehend, viscerally, on the gut level I mean, that it goes far beyond that. When people picture the dinosaur or ice ages for example, they mentally people it with those strange animals, or glaciers, but keep everything else pretty much the same, oceans, blue skies, puffy white clouds. Most of us don't take into account that even the air would be different. For example, the oxygen levels during the Carboniferous period would have been much higher than now. Fires would have ignited quickly, and burned ferociously. Moreover, there is strong evidence for microbial life forms living as far back as 3.85 billion years ago. Prokaryotes, single-celled life forms without a nucleus, may have also existed; yet dangerous viruses or bacteria only rarely come up in sci-fi stories and seldom in time travel tales. Why not? And an ice age is nothing compared to a Snowball Earth, when the entire planet was white, low in oxygen because of little plant life, but getting ever higher in its carbon dioxide mixture. You wouldn't be able to even breathe there.

There were many times in the past, and there will be again in the future, when our planet was, or will be, fundamentally and totally alien to us, so different, we wouldn't probably recognize it as ours. If you were somehow transported to those eras, you would probably believe you were on another planet altogether.

It wouldn't just be the animals romping around that would make you think this, or how hot or cold it was; it would be just about everything, every aspect of what you think of as familiar would be different—plants, animals, terrain, even the skies and the stars in them. I'm betting you'd find that planet incredibly hostile and strange, and probably unsafe and/or unfit for colonization by humans.

How different could it be? Well, for instance, a few million years either way would make the heavens appear utterly different to us, with a multitude of unfamiliar stars forming strange constellations. Judging by them, we wouldn't even be able to tell if we were on our own world then. Planets might well have been in different orbits, looked very different. Something big happened to Uranus, for instance. And even a Mars-like world probably crashed into the Earth at one point. And as for Mars, at one time, it may have looked much like Earth—a blue world instead of red.

And, depending on whether you went forward or backward in time, the moon would be closer or farther away. It might disappear altogether; look different, without its mares, totally different patterns of craters. Or it might eventually wander away from earth altogether billions of years from now, or come crashing down on us in the far future.

We do know the moon is receding from the Earth at close to 1.5 inches a year, and so once was much closer. So, travel back far enough in time and you will have a bloated moon with a different-looking face suspended above you, filling the night and day sky, causing tides that would yank the land out from under you, as high as a kilometer before dropping it back, and thus causing numerous tremors at the top of the Richter scale. Go far enough into the future, and the moon will be so far away that it will appear tiny, a bright speck in the sky. Our day will be longer, and tides virtually nonexistent.

Several billion years from now, the moon will be 1.6 times farther away than it is at present. Its period of revolution will be about 55 days. Eventually, our world's rotation will take fifty-five days (same tidal friction problems) and thus the moon may appear to stay in one place forever, hanging over just one portion of our planet. Anyone living on the wrong side of the planet would have to travel far to see the moon hanging in the sky. You see, only beings living in certain regions, but nowhere else on Earth, could see it. Can you imagine how strange this would seem to people alive today? Try visualizing living on an Earth where one day is equal to fifty-five of ours, and it only takes seven of them to make a whole year.

The weather would be awful, too, on such an Earth. There would be intense heating on the sun side, terrific cooling and freezing on the other. Violent winds would be one probable outcome. Migrating oceans might be another. Oh, and don't forget to throw in a couple billion years of evolution (if life survives that long), and you would have an Earth unknown to us, one that is truly alien, indeed! Even the sun would be much larger and a different color—a brilliant red.

So if we travel far enough through time either way, we end up on a planet that seems nothing like our own. Length of day, temperatures, landmasses, atmospheric constituents (or none at all), size and proximity of moon (or whether we even see or have one), tides, weather, life forms, unrecognizable star patterns, strange plants and animals—all of it will be in the future, or was already in the past, vastly different from what we know today. Great places and times to set stories in then, aren't they? (Who needs other planets when you have ever-changing Earth?)

How about changes occurring now? There is global warming and the possibility of a sudden ice age onset (another Big Chill?), but what about other things? Did you know, for example, that on any given day there are about twenty-four volcanoes in an erupting phase? In the past, so many volcanoes let go at once that they severely altered the constituents of the atmosphere. They produced lava fields that covered thousands of square miles (so-called Siberian Traps) and caused major biological die-offs, perhaps the biggest one in Earth's history. Think of the stories you could write if this were to start happening again—now?

And this isn't even taking into account super volcanoes. These monsters do not often erupt, but when they do, the consequences are chilling. The Yellowstone Caldera in Yellowstone Park, Wyoming, is one example. For a long time we didn't even know it existed. It wasn't until NASA wanted to test some heat sensing equipment that we realized the caldera was even there.

Visitors walked around Yellowstone every day, enjoying the geysers and boiling mud pots, not the least bit aware they were perched precariously atop an active super volcano. Many geologists consider it to be (currently) the most dangerous one on Earth! It erupts about once every six hundred thousand years or so. That means it is due any time now for another such eruption. And remember, many scientists believe one such super volcano, about 70,000 or so years ago, reduced the human population on the entire planet to a mere few thousand! Again, this is an excellent idea for a story setting.

If the Yellowstone Caldera blows, it will mean total devastation for hundreds of square miles around, sending tons upon tons of soil and debris high into the atmosphere. This debris will make the nuclear blast at Hiroshima look like a child's pop-gun toy by comparison. A nuclear-style winter will engulf the Earth. Plant life will suffer and die, and then the rest of the food chain (meaning us) will, too.

Ash up to five inches deep could cover the United States and most of Canada from coast to coast. Much deeper layers of ash (feet thick) will plaster enormous areas of North America, wreaking havoc on the Great Plains breadbasket. (Word of advice: should Yellowstone go off, run don't walk to your nearest supermarket and stock up on those canned goods! Trust me; you'll need them.) Is that enough of an alien planet for you?

Earth is hardly static. Transformations are happening all the time. Our planet careens from one wild swing to another, suffering numerous and swift changes that have catastrophic results for life on land, and in the seas. Some scientists, for instance, now think that ice ages might come in mere decades, instead of over centuries. Changes on this alien Earth are always occurring and every day.

They make great concepts for stories with settings and plots limited only by a writer's imagination. Whether it is an author setting his or her stories in the beginning of time, Devonian period, Dinosaur Age, Ice Ages, far future, or just a few decades from now, Earth is the perfect alien planet for your story. Think about it. And it isn't just science fiction. Many major fantasy authors have used past ages of Earth for their settings.

Next time, we'll discuss truly alien worlds, how to create them, and how not to mess it up big time when doing so! When building planets from scratch, one has to be very careful!

CHAPTER 8

Painted Black?—Creating "Atmospheres" For Your Stories

"The days were dim, relentlessly gloomy. Decades had passed since anyone had seen a blue sky, a warm yellow sun. There was no real rain either, just the constant drip of stagnant water in countless dark corners, the black liquid pooling in numerous dank alleys. The teeming throngs of the metropolis surged and ebbed through a myriad of these narrow wet streets. They were just so many faceless shadows flowing, anonymous silhouettes, streaming. More like insects than people, they all scuttled about like roaches in their mindless millions, eating, breeding, but barely surviving for very long."

Yes, it's a scenario very analogous to that of the movie, **Blade Runner**, and similar to the settings of any number of other science fiction movies/stories—right? But no, before you think or say it, my purpose with this illustration isn't to knock those stories or movies for painting their settings all in shades of black. I don't care that they are negative scenarios, opposite to more positive futures, such as ones used in shows like the various **Star Trek** series and movies.

What I do care about is if they are believable scenarios, realistically portrayed with convincing atmospheres that are appropriate to the story. Because they set the tone for your story, tell the reader what to expect. In essence, atmosphere makes the story in many respects. Furthermore, for those who want to "say something," politically, socially, or otherwise, atmosphere is all important for getting your point across. So, we're going to stray just a little at this point to illustrate this idea, of atmosphere and mood creating better settings for not only our stories themselves, but what we want to say in them.

Now, consider this quotation:

"*Oh brave new world, that has such people in it*"

—William Shakespeare, *The Tempest.*

John, a prominent character in Aldous Huxley's novel, *Brave New World*, quotes the above line. Huxley, of course, stole it from Shakespeare. Don't writers just love to steal from each other? Ray Bradbury once told me that it's the best way to become a writer. Steal from others, but not as a plagiarist, instead as a means to acquire new ideas and concepts, then to transform them, and thus transmute it into your own work.

In any case, Huxley used Shakespeare's quotation because his character, John, felt he was embarking on just such an adventure, one to a brave, new, and marvelous world, and one that sounded ideal, even utopian to him. What did he find when he actually reached that marvelous future London? Nothing good! This makes the irony of that quote even more compelling. It also illustrates how one's expectations can exceed reality by a wide margin, a point driven home with gritty determination by Aldous Huxley in his novel.

That future world, as painted by Huxley, was one of high technology. To paraphrase, it was a joyful place, but one which knew no real joy or love. Conditioned from birth, and manipulated physically and emotionally to feel happy, its people lived in a dismal unfeeling society, one that was immensely rigid in structure.

The inhabitants were not much more than unwitting automatons culturally imbued with the need to perform certain types of tasks, and those tasks only. When reality intruded too much, the authorities freely and widely distributed the drug, soma. It was a euphoric narcotic.

Of course, too much soma brought on physical collapse and an early death, but that wasn't a problem. They just brought the children into the death wards so they could see that dying was no big deal (whether or not it really was). Why change the circumstances when you can just change people's innate reactions to them? So much simpler—the perfect answer to everything.

Charming vision of the future, isn't it? But that's what science fiction writers do. We paint landscapes of tomorrow with moods and atmosphere, and then we people them with characters, plots, and events. And let's be honest here; we don't do it just to entertain. Aldous Huxley didn't. You see, he wrote *Brave New World* in 1932. It was a time of intense social change, economic upheaval, and the rise of fascism and communism just across the English Channel in Europe. Frightened for the future of humanity, he created a novel to illustrate the dangers, to point out the wrong paths that societies must take care not to follow.

Later, George Orwell did the same thing with his book, *Animal Farm*, and again with his appallingly chilling novel, *1984*. Oh, and if you are prone to think that these are just silly, out-of-date novels, and no longer relevant; don't! They keep printing new editions and make them into movies, and not just once, but repeatedly, because they *do* have lasting value.

Warnings usually do. And they bear repeating. One such example of this, as recently as last season on the Sci-Fi Channel, was yet another version of *Brave New World*. (It wasn't the best version I've ever seen, by the way.) So even today, many people feel such novels must have value. What they say is still important and needs hearing.

As writers, we all do this to some greater or lesser degree, don't we? That is, we describe our personal visions of possible futures? Moreover, we put in much of what we personally feel about politics, current social conditions, and religions. In other words, we have our say about things, comment on the state of affairs, and certain trends. We raise warning flags about the future. We try to offer opinions, cautions, and guidance. In short, we try to influence the way events will turn out.

Can anyone doubt, for instance, what Arthur C. Clarke of *2001, A Space Odyssey* fame, thought about religion? I'll bet you anything he was an atheist, or at the very least, an agnostic. His novels ring with such opinions, and they are negative ones where religions are concerned. It's clear he didn't think that religious beliefs are so much the "opiate of the masses," as Karl Marx stated, but instead he thought of them as superstitious holdovers from primitive times. For him, such beliefs were just drawbacks, or obstacles to our continued progress. At least, that seems to have been his view.

If you need more proof of writers stating their political and social views, just pick up some old issues of *Analog*. There was one story there about hippies taking over the world and the intelligent people (e.g., scientists, engineers, pilots) fleeing to the moon, struggling to get there against great odds. The young hippies didn't want them to go, you see, and they controlled access. They went to extreme lengths to stop the brain drain. Does that tell you what the author thought of hippies at the time, and where such "bizarre" behavior might lead if allowed to continue its course unchecked? I think so! And Analog is full of such types of stories, year after year. Warnings all, and warnings raised by authors about everything one can imagine, from religion to cloning, abortion to racism—you name it—it's all there.

Okay, okay, so the secret is out. We all do it, big names, as well as small-fry writers. So how can we do it without coming across like political pundits and/or table-pounding extremists?

Well, there is that old writing adage, "show, don't tell." It particularly applies here. Instead of having a character on a soapbox spouting your viewpoints in your future landscape, paint your feelings in with specific events that illustrate your points. Your descriptions will set the tone, as well. That's extremely important.

Atmosphere, mood "shows" the reader what you feel about your future world without some character having to "tell" them. Here's a good example of this from the opening paragraph of *Brave New World*:

> "*A SQUAT grey building of only thirty-four stories. Over the main entrance the words, CENTRAL LONDON HATCHERY AND CONDITION- ING CENTRE, and, in a shield, the World State's*

motto, COMMUNITY,   IDENTITY,   STA-BILITY."

You see? The first two lines of his book set the tone, thus the mood, in clear and concise terms. It immediately tells the reader what is most important in that world. That is, community, identity, stability. These ideals then, are paramount in Huxley's vision, over self-expression, freedom, charity, true love, and hosts of other things that we feel are so necessary in our lives today. And don't forget that word "CONDITIONING." It immediately lets the reader know something unsavory is happening. Do notice he capitalizes entire words. It makes them leap out at the reader, and screams "significant point here!"

George Orwell's, *1984*, is even more grim and gray. It is a world that, frankly, I would rather die than live in, with its Stalin-like leaders, miserable living conditions, endless wars, thought-police, and all the rest. It is a true dystopia. But there is no mistaking the somber mood. It endures, virtually nonstop, throughout the entire work. And that mood tells you precisely how the author feels about such a reality.

Anyway, once you have set the mood, maintain it throughout your story, or as long as needed to get the point across. Make events in your plot actively illustrate whatever kind of future you feel it is to be.

Are thought-police sensing your characters' dread secrets in an "Orwellian" future? Is Captain Kirk trying to preserve a peace-loving Federation against a grasping "evil empire?" And don't forget the dark dripping world of *Blade Runner*, with its dire warnings on multiple subjects.

Environmental degradation aside, though, I think the point of that novel was to question the definition of what it is that makes us human. Furthermore, it asks under what circumstances that definition may become confused or lost. Again, which opinions one stresses in a story are all entirely up to the individual writer.

One final, but important point, and I can't stress this enough; writers have tremendous power over their readership. It is far more subtle than people realize. Psychological experiments and studies have shown that people who are very against something, and who then read information about the opposite viewpoint from their own, will immediately reject it out of hand. At first!

As time goes by, it is also an established point that those same people will start quoting facts and statements from the very thing that they themselves initially and utterly rejected. Time, apparently, distances people from the disagreeable source of facts and ideas; their minds then make it okay to use and even accept some of them. They then incorporate them into their opinions and worldview. Conditioning, anyone?

So as writers, our statements on all sorts of issues have immense power to sway people, if not right away, then in the near future. And that's the whole point, isn't it, to do just that? But be careful with such power. As the Master said in the television series, *Kung Fu*, "use it wisely, little grasshopper!" For science fiction writers, it just may be that truer words were never spoken!

And now that we've discussed how to get ideas, create settings, and atmosphere, let's move on to how we get our own voice and style. Just how important is it, and how hard is it to acquire our own style?

CHAPTER 9

Style, Voice,

The Basic Principles Of Story Telling

Frustration can be a terrible thing, especially with regard to developing one's own writing ability, finding a voice, and style that suits us as individuals. I'm sure we've all experienced this as science fiction, fantasy, or horror authors, if not on a regular basis, then perhaps at some point near the beginning of our careers. This can also happen later on, when we flex our artistic writing muscles in a new direction. When we try innovative endeavors, attempt to forge a new style, it can get very aggravating if we don't succeed in the way we wish. To be denied our instant gratification can be a terrible and traumatizing thing, apparently...

What's also annoying is when we are called upon to critique other people's work, and something absolutely horrible leaps out at us, a gross violation of basic principles of writing, as it were. I'm not talking minor stuff here, like ending sentences with prepositions, using slang or jargon in narrative, that sort of trifling thing. We all do that, sometimes for the very sake of our style. I'm referring to the BIG MISTAKES, the kind that leaps out at one and makes you, as a reader, stop dead in your tracks and marvel at the sheer audacity, or perhaps rather the incomparable ignorance of that particular author.

I've had this happen to me often, since I'm a member of several reciprocating critique organizations where we review each other's work. And when one carefully mentions such a glaring error of basic writing to the appropriate author, sometimes, many times in fact, they scream "but that's my style!" I guess they feel that allows them *carte blanche* to commit such ghastly gaffes. It seems, sadly, to be a coverall excuse for any mistakes and/or omissions on their part.

So here's my question; does it really? Does style make it all okay; cover a multitude of editorial sins and transgressions? Are we allowed to change anything, do anything, in the name of developing our own peculiar writing style? Can we, as authors, negate basic rules, ignore primary writing precepts, twist and turn grammar around in order to find our individual voice? And having then found it; I wonder, would anyone then want to listen to it under such extreme circumstances?

Moreover, why does this seem to be such a commonality among writers these days, seemingly being the rule among newer authors, rather than the rare exception?

Well, first of all, I think this situation is born, to some degree, from desperation and ignorance. Let's be honest here, our educational system, nationwide, has fallen on very hard times. It's been this way for years now. On the national news just this last week, it said that 32 percent of Americans tested couldn't pass an American Citizenship Test!?! Over 40 percent of high school seniors couldn't locate the United States on a world map! And as a former tech writer, we were told in no uncertain terms that according to tests of the time, the average graduate engineer and doctor read at a 7th grade level, so that's the level we had to write at for them! Incredible, isn't it?

So, it is a fact that the average reading ability of college-graduating engineers, doctors, and other professionals is now at or near the seventh grade reading level. Even this level has been falling of late. I'm also a technical writer, so I know this. I've been told, unequivocally, that I must write manuals for neurosurgeon brain scanner equipment at the seventh or preferably even the sixth grade level! Really, isn't that a frightening thought when one considers how much we may be relying upon a particular neurosurgeon to take care of us? I mean, can they even read the instruction manual for their own equipment correctly enough to use it properly on us? Uh-Oh!

So new and apparently often under-educated authors (when it comes to knowing how to write or even read properly), may become impatient, want to leap ahead and despite their lack of basic writing skills, and take a quantum leap from novice to supposed adept, without understanding that they must go through the middle process of first learning to write well. They simply don't realize that they don't yet know how to do this, even when editors consistently tell them so. (*"But it's my style,"* *they wail.*)

Certainly, I freely admit that not all authors are in this boat of leaking illiteracy. Many may already have a good background in writing ability when they begin to write fiction, or they then struggle on, correcting themselves constantly along the way, and ultimately achieving their goal of finding an efficacious style and ability through sheer hard work, and often stultifying perseverance. That last has been my route.

Others, however, try to hurry things along a little by taking workshops, doing quick and intense crash courses, such as the *Clarion Workshop.* These have good success rates, by the way, but beware; the instructor can be brutal (necessarily so, I think), in order to accomplish their goals in the time provided them. Still, other writers join free critiquing groups that reciprocate with each other, as I have done. These also can work very well if given the chance. And they are far cheaper—being free for the most part.

Any or all of these things, in my opinion, are helpful, and among the right things a would-be author should consider doing. Writers taking these routes show they are serious, are trying to learn their craft, are striving to be better at them, are honing their skills, and in doing so, often are truly becoming much better writers. After all, a carpenter must first know how to use the tools of his trade, sharpen his skills, before he can make anything of beauty or of lasting consequence—right? Well, it works the same for authors.

I think the problem for many well-meaning writers is when they totally ignore the critiques or reviews they do receive, whether these come from their own writing peer groups, editors (often in the form of rejections), or otherwise.

Yes, this sort of response on the author's part does happen and frequently. Ego has a lot to do with this. It's not easy having someone rip apart a story you think is great. Trust me in this; I know! Painful isn't the word. So, rather than accept the criticism as valid, the writer derides the source, diminishing it, claiming that the reviewer(s) just didn't understand what the author was trying to accomplish.

Yeah, right! Maybe those authors should realize that if a professional editor or fellow writer has a hard time comprehending what the author is trying to accomplish with their story, then maybe the average reader would have even a harder time? Hmm, maybe?

So let's restate the problem; we have many writers whose mechanical skills at their craft may be sadly lacking in many respects. Being new in the field, they may not even realize this problem, since they are the victims of a not-so-hot educational system, which tells them that since they have graduated (college?), they are qualified to write.

Then compound this with problems of ego, which can result in defensive behaviors, their protective shields going up, so to speak, and an intense desire to have a style all their own, and to stand out in a growing crowd. And what do you have? No, not a temperamental writer wrapped in cotton wool, at least not in the literal sense, but rather someone who simply has missed the point, doesn't understand what is required to be a good author. They are just drifting, perhaps blaming others, but never themselves. And neither are they getting published!

What are some major slip-ups in trying to create a personal style? Well, purple prose is high on my list of things to be avoided. I recently reviewed a story where an author referred to someone running on foot at a normal rate of speed, and heading directly into a wall. When the character hit the obstruction, the author said their "bones evaporated." Another author said that some pond smelled "musty" and "green." What???? As far as I'm concerned, that tale also read "purple!" How in the hell does something smell "green?" Chartreuse, maybe—that's a joke!

I know we all want an individual style, readily recognizable, but juxtaposing adjectives, verbs, and nouns together at random just isn't the way to go. Another author I critiqued had the tremendously annoying habit of doing one-line paragraphs. I'm not talking dialogue here, which should be set out that way when necessary, but rather simple narrative.

He wrote like this.

He did this not just once in a while, but all the time.

I'm not kidding.

Really!

The author drove me crazy by the end of the story.

No, really again!

I never knew who was talking because of this. The novel sucked!

See what I mean? Now, I'm not picking on these particular authors, and they shall remain nameless, but when one resorts to these extremes to create one's own style, then they've gone too far in my considered opinion. Major and constant disruptions of grammar and syntax for no valid reason, interruptions in narrative flow just in order to create a personal voice or style, simply are not acceptable. By this, I don't mean that one can't get away with it once in a while, or that it might not be valid for some dramatic effect in a particular story or context, but just to do it as a constant "style" won't work, not for the reader. Once burned by this, they'll avoid such authors like the plague. Rightly so, in my opinion.

We have grammar and vocabulary rules for a reason, like it or not. It's so that we can all read each other's stuff and basically understand it. Such rules form a common framework by which we all abide, so we can comprehend and communicate with each other at a reasonable level.

Failure to at least give some lip service to this framework is to invite failure, real and enduring failure, as an author. Major and constant deviations from the standard rules, whether intentional or committed out of ignorance, won't work with the editors who have to plow through such purple prose, or obtuse stabs at grammar and literature, and it certainly won't work well with the reader. Trust me, they have a very short attention span, and the limits of their patience are even shorter! Make the readers work too hard at reading your story and you will lose them. They'll simply stop reading and move on to something else. Let's be honest; we've all done this at one time or another, haven't we? Who hasn't picked up a novel or story only to later put it down again still unfinished, and permanently so?

So my advice, for what it's worth, is that even if you think you are an accomplished writer, that you still know or learn at least the basics of grammar, style, and vocabulary. Periodically, double-check yourself on these issues. Seek out websites, books, and essays on writing. Read them on occasion. Absorb them. Use them. Apply their principles. See if you are still following, at least basically, their main points.

And don't strive so hard to create a personal style or voice through the use of purple prose, non-sequitur nonsense statements such as, "I smelled a delicate shade of blue wafting on the heckling breeze," or by fundamentally flawed stylistic changes in sentence and paragraph structures, just for the heck of it. Editors will spot this in a New York minute! They won't like it.

Let your style evolve naturally. First just tell the story. Then allow your voice to grow of its own accord, without undue pressure and/or time constraints. It will, you know, and it will be a better voice for having evolved naturally, rather than having been acquired through some artificial overlay of contrived writing methods, and ones which are then usually inferior, as a result.

In other words, have some faith in yourself that you can grow over time as an author. After all, if we aren't always growing in this way, then we are stagnant, have reached a plateau, haven't we? And what's that old saying, "Those who do not move forward must inevitably fall behind?" As authors, we want to avoid this particular trap. We can do this by constantly trying to improve our writing skills.

In the final analysis, writing, any writing, science fiction, fantasy, horror, or otherwise, is a craft, a learned set of skills. Develop these. Refine them. Use the tools freely provided everywhere for this purpose. Then apply this writing ability to tell your stories. Your style will come automatically, and over time.

But remember, if you think the answer as a new author is to just jump in, without having attempted to learn the rudiments of writing, then you are in for a rude surprise. Readers won't like your work. Also importantly, neither will editors. Don't believe me? Check out editorial guideline sites for many publishers. Not only do they stress good quality writing, error free as possible, but they even list websites where one can go to learn how to do these things. Some even list the basics of good grammar right there that they want you to use. Now, would editors go to the trouble of having that in their guidelines if it wasn't a major issue for them, if they didn't want it done? Ignore them and their advice at your own peril.

Oh, and if you notice any grammar, vocabulary, or other flaws in this chapter, please just ignore them. After all, it's perfectly okay for me to write this way, since it's my particular STYLE! Meanwhile, I'm going to go for a purple swim now, paddle through a field of effervescent stones until they evaporate and I can taste the essence of the color blue misting off them in a heady perfume of positive trend! Hey, that's my style! So that makes it absolutely okay to write this way, right? Wrong!

CHAPTER 10

Creating Characters In Science Fiction—I Need A Hero!

Well, don't we all—at some point, don't we need a hero in our lives? Let's face it, at sometime, somehow, in someway; we want a hero to save us, even if it's only from the dull tasks of our daily drudgery, the binds of our own tedious existence (or is this just me? YIKES!). The character, Lois Lane, for instance, just loves Superman to grab her up and whisk her away on a regular basis. Even Jimmy, cub reporter, seemed to enjoy this. Hmm…is this an as-yet unseen facet to Superman's character, or Jimmy's? Inquiring minds want to know! I'm just joking. But we do need heroes, and especially when writing in science fiction, fantasy (particularly), and horror.

It seems we need someone to defy the gods, challenge evil, and conquer fate. There is an innate need for that which is greater than we are, someone with whom we can identify in some small way, perceive as a symbol of hope, look up to, and perhaps to some minor extent, even emulate.

Heroes are important to us. There is no doubt about it. That's been a truism throughout history. It's just as true today. For instance, modern life has spawned a plethora of comic books, all with their various heroes doing the impossible, or at least, improbable. From the Silver Surfer, The Phantom, Batman, Superman, Green Lantern, Flash, The Torch, Wonder Woman, Thor, and so on (the list is almost endless these days), heroes spring forth to save us, as individuals and humanity as a whole. Oh, yes—we need our heroes! We always have and I think we always will, especially in story telling.

The idea of the hero, the hero concept, or myth, forms a

bedrock basis of almost every culture's first forms of literature, or is usually fundamental to them, as in the hero-myth epic. Such great myth epics as Scandinavia's *Beowulf,* or Old Babylonia's *Gilgamesh,* and Homer's Greek epics, *The Iliad* and *The Odyssey,* are good examples of these and there are lots more where those come from. Even the bible has such types of people in it. Moses, for example, heroically leads the entire nation of the Israelites out of Egypt. Noah is another example of a biblical hero, as is Joshua. Now, whether or not we believe in these heroes as fact or fiction is not the point here. That's for each individual to decide. My argument here is that it seems we do need that role model, that hero, real or imagined, and not just on an individual level, but even as nations, peoples.

However, because of the overwhelmingly masculine heritage and emotional baggage, the term "hero" provokes, I think, right off the bat, we do need some clarification about this term. First, let's look at a *definition of "hero." Webster's Dictionary defines it as:*

> *"**Main Entry:***
>
> *he ro...*
>
> *Etymology:*
>
> *Latin heros, from Greek* hērōs
>
> *Date: 14th century*
>
> *1 a: a mythological or legendary figure often of divine descent endowed with great strength or ability b: an illustrious warrior c: a man admired for his achievements and noble qualities d: one that shows great courage*
>
> *2 a: the principal male character in a literary or dramatic work b: the central figure in an event, period, or movement*
>
> *3:* plural usually *heros...*
>
> *4: an object of extreme admiration and devotion: idol"*

I think that's all self-explanatory, and it certainly defines the "hero" in a very masculine way. Now let's look at the definition of a "heroine." Wordnet defines a "heroine" as:

> *"n 1: the main good female character in a work of fiction; 2: a woman possessing heroic qualities."*

Please note how insipid the female "heroine" definition is when compared to that of "hero." A "good female"—how pathetic is that? I think some dictionaries could use a little revision, because they aren't keeping up with the times! So it is with regard to these two disparate definitions, "hero" versus "heroine," that I'm personally going to differ on definitions with those stated above.

From now on, for purposes of this article, when I use the word "hero," I'm going to mean either male or female, interchangeably, and I mean the first definition, that of "hero," (as defined above), rather than just the more meager version of a "heroine." Why am I doing this in contradiction to a dictionary? Well, because I think the use of "heroine," as defined in such a way, is woefully inadequate in today's world. In just the last couple of decades, great changes have occurred in this literary regard, although they've been happening to some degree all along.

Our idea of a "heroine" has undergone dramatic modifications. All we have to do is look around to see that there are now numerous female characters, such as Laura Croft of **Tomb Raider** fame, that fit the historical definition of "hero," more closely, rather than the much weaker one of "heroine." In fact, many editors don't even like to use the term, "heroine," anymore, feeling it is an archaic expression, and so opt instead for just using one word, "hero."

Heck, we do the same thing with the word "actor," don't we? It now seems to include both the male and female genders. Ah well, times change, as the cliché goes, and sometimes for the better in this case. We authors have to change with them!

Okay, so now that we have a good working definition of what a "hero" is, some other questions need answering. For instance, do we still need them in modern science fiction, fantasy, or horror, or will some other form of character(s) do as well?

Have heroes undergone such radical changes over the years that they no longer fit the dictionary definitions at all? Are they changing beyond recognition? And what about the much heralded and vaunted rise of the "anti-hero" that became so popular in the 60's, 70's, 80's, and 90's? Are they still with us? Are anti-heroes taking over? Are science fiction heroes taking this direction, heading toward being protagonists still, but lacking in most heroic qualities, such as courage?

See, there are many questions! So, let's see if we can't answer them. First, with regard to heroes existing in modern science fiction, fantasy, and yes, horror, as well—are they still there? Oh yes, they most definitely are! They exist in many forms and in lots of disguises, but they are still there. Many categories of them exist. For instance, we have the wimps that transform through some means or other (for a movie example, see, Jim Carrey in **The Mask**). Yep, those average persons who somehow become greater through circumstances beyond their control, either by some hidden strength from within, or in the classic style of epic myth, given some strength from without, as a mask from the god, Loki. That approach, by the way, follows the tradition of many original epic myths almost perfectly. Most ancient heroes were bestowed with special powers by the gods.

Now, back to the hidden strength type of hero, one of our favorites, it seems. These are ones, who through some means, such as tremendous adversity (as in the movie, **Gladiator**), have that hidden strength awakened. What qualities they had before become magnified, honed, sharpened, greater, as a result. "Steely determination" often is one of these attributes. This is often brought about by a need for revenge and/or vengeance.

As for anti-heroes, yes, they still abound in science fiction and we, as authors, use them often. The reluctant hero, as it were, who must do good things whether they want to or not, because of some greater power or problem hanging over them. It's as if the author has them blackmailed into doing well, whether they want to or not. Of course, deep down inside, we know they are good people; they have been just terribly hurt somewhere along the line. Ah well…life is tough! Since we're using comic book heroes often here, let's stick with that. Think, *The Hulk,* or the

Swamp Creature. Those tragic figures, forced into doing well, when all they wanted was a "normal" life.

Then we have sort of the group hero thingy. This is where a number of people band together, each with certain positive traits, who together strive to overcome the odds, as sort of a group hero. Think *Fantastic Four.* This is a perfect example. Each character has different traits (exaggerated for comic book purposes—in sci-fi, we tone those down usually quite a bit, but fantasies and "pure" horror don't' have to). Each character also has different flaws. Usually, though, authors include one character who acts as sort of the mind and heart of the group, the diplomat so to speak, that keeps the group cohesive.

Now again, in science fiction, our characters are generally much more subtle than comic book characters, but not always. Many times we have a character undergo some transformation that gives them enormous power, such as ESP, prophetic visions, some chance discovery they can use to their advantage, etc. Fantasy does this as well, usually through some magical device, such as a sword, amulet, ring, or as a gift from some sort of divine personage. Horror can bestow special attributes on a hero through some terrible means (lab accidents, strange occurrences, etc.).

And as always, our heroes should be believable. Comic book characters are fine, but even among those, we tend to identify more with the ones that have some human aspects remaining to them, like *Spiderman.* Even our big heroes need weaknesses. *Superma"* has kryptonite, and an endless string of women he cares about whose names always include two "L's." Achilles, of epic myth proportions, had that "Achilles heel" of which we hear about all the time. So remember, when you, as an author, are creating a hero, keep this in mind. They must have their strengths, but heroes must also have their weaknesses. Otherwise, they'll be two-dimensional, two "comic book" to be believed in your stories.

Audiences today are more sophisticated in this regard, than they once were. They want heroes, certainly, but they expect them to be three-dimensional. So, do keep this in mind.

CHAPTER 11

The Elements Of Horror

When is something a true horror story? Under what conditions can a tale be one of pure horror or horror with just science fiction and/or fantasy as a mere backdrop? And when might something be a genuine science fiction tale with just some horror added in it?

Hard questions and there are many answers, but all with their own attendant problems. You see, as with all genre writing, things get a little fuzzy when you near those vague borders of any genre land. What constitutes what? Is H.P. Lovecraft pure horror with a science fiction overlay, or vice versa—that is, a sci-fi genre with strong elements of horror? After all, he did create an alien mythos as the background and basis for his Cthulu stories. This same sort of thing, to varying degrees, applies to such authors as Edgar Allen Poe, Stephen King, Dean Koontz, and so many others. They all write or wrote horror, but to some degree, science fiction as well, and sometimes sci-fi with strong horror aspects.

But which is which? When do they cross over from horror into science fiction with a strong horror element? Are the Stephen King novels, *Tommy Knockers*, and *Dream Catcher*, horror stories basically, or science fiction with horror in them? Sometimes it's clear; **The_Shining,** by Stephen King, is pure horror. But other times we're not certain at all.

For instance, let's take a quick glance at a case in point; the movie, **Alien**, seems a perfect example of this type of question. Here, crewmembers aboard a space freighter discover aliens on an alien world—detestable creatures! They inadvertently bring one back aboard ship (sort of as an intestinal parasite from hell!), whereupon it grows, gets loose, wreaks havoc, kills everybody, and only one person (played by the actress, Sigourney Weaver), survives long enough to escape in a life pod, along with her little kitty cat.

Is this a science fiction story with strong horror elements? On the face of it, it would appear so, but let's dissect it a little. First, one must ask if science fiction is a necessary requirement for this tale. And the answer, superficially, would seem to be yes. The story needs an alien setting for the monster to come from, right? They have to have a ship isolated in space upon which for it to commit mayhem, and then there is the self-destruct mechanism for the freighter (counting down as always to build suspense, shades of the movie, **Andromeda Strain**), and finally our hero's escape with said pussycat into deep space with both of them in cryogenic sleep.

But could not this story work just as well on, say, a sailing vessel at sea? And instead, could the alien just be a monstrous entity from the deep ocean or from the supernatural (as in the movie, **The Fog**)? Could the solution be to sink the vessel along with the monster? Our hero could just as easily make her escape (with that annoying little "puddy tat") in a lifeboat, couldn't she? And yeah, if you want to be accurate, the monster could be hiding under a tarp on the lifeboat, waiting for our hero to push it overboard. Does it sound similar to the movie? It is, but it isn't science fiction. And that's my point.

Another question; was the alien believable as a true sci-fi alien, or is it really just a horror-style monster? Let's be honest here, an alien that evolves with acid for blood, a sliding jaw full of endless teeth, has the universe's weirdest procreation system (using, what are to it, totally alien hosts in order for it to reproduce), and can withstand the cold vacuum of interstellar space for long periods seems a bit much. Well, come on…doesn't it?

What planet did this nasty little critter come from that had such extreme natural conditions on it? How could such a severe world evolve life at all? Did the planet have many alien visitors—

enough to allow evolution to figure them into a permanent system of reproduction for a species? If not, could a closed ecosystem evolve a creature so well suited for reproducing off world, so ultimately malignant, and oh yeah, so frightfully intelligent? Not really very likely, is it?

So given these factors, the movie, **Alien**, might well be considered a true horror story that just used a science fiction backdrop. Or to some people, ones who feel strongly enough that the science fiction elements were essential to the story's success, perhaps it is genuine sci-fi. I personally don't think that, but that's just my opinion. I think it was a darn good horror movie. It scared me!

But there you have the point I've been trying to make. The line between something being true horror and something being science fiction with horror in it, is a thin one. It's open to interpretation. But there are definite questions we can ask ourselves when writing to help us find the answers to this conundrum of which is which. So, how do we write successful SF with horror, or strong horror elements in it?

1. We have to follow the basic rules of writing a good story. That's primary whether your story is science fiction, fantasy, or a true "pure" horror story. We've discussed the rules for this already, in the very first chapter on the five basic steps to getting published. so let's just say a good science fiction, fantasy, or horror story must first just be a good story, adhering to the age-old guidelines for such.

2. If the story is to be a true horror science fiction tale, then the story must first be true science fiction. That is, the setting/backdrops, the plot, and characters must all interact and depend principally on the science fiction aspects of the tale in order to work. If the story can exist without the science fiction aspects, then it is not dependent on them, and thus is not truly science fiction. It is just a story with a science fiction background or overlay. An example; a serial murderer loose aboard a passenger starship would probably work just as well aboard an earthly luxury liner at sea in just about any period of modern history, so that wouldn't really need science fiction to work, unless the author depends on some bit of science fiction as crucial for the plot to unfold.

3. To be a sci-fi horror story, the horror must work in the sci-fi story. Taking a true science fiction tale, and just doing an overlay of horror aspects to it, isn't really doing the job right. The horror, just as it would be in a "pure" horror story, must come across as real, integral, a part of the very tale itself. It must seem profound, intrinsic, and frightening to the reader. And above all, it must rely heavily on the science fiction aspects of the story to be able to work.

But what, exactly, is horror? There are many definitions, but the things that make for a good horror plot, whether in "pure" horror, sci-fi, or fantasy are all the same and usually must involve these factors:

a. An unknown quantity. This must exist as something that instigates the fear, acts as, or is the source for it. It must come from either without or within, but its source should be unknown, uncertain, and the nature of the danger, its real magnitude, must be equally uncertain, at least in the beginning of the plot. What's more, this evil must be only slowly and carefully revealed throughout the tale. If it is revealed in its entirety up front, then the story must be about how the characters attempt to combat it.

b. Isolation. A sense of isolation is absolutely paramount! The victim(s) must feel isolated from the rest of humanity in some way, and so stranded from any real help. **In short, they must feel helpless.** This can be isolation in the middle of nowhere, or the heart of a city, but the victim(s) should feel helpless, left to face the coming evil and combat it on their own. Think of all of Stephen King's stories, how they so often are set in the middle of empty rural areas in winter, cabins in snowstorms, or raging blizzards, where the characters become geographically and physically isolated, cut off from any real help.

Other authors and movie creators often do this by putting characters in some solitary spaceship (e.g., the movies, **Supernova**, and/or **Event Horizon**), fortress (the older but frightening movie, **The Keep**), or big old house (remember the movie version of **Rose Red?**), ones that are geographically or otherwise isolated by locking in their victims. Notice, I use movies here as examples? The truth is they make very good examples, because they are so visually explicit in this regard. They "show" the isolation that a writer needs to create for horror in any of its genre forms.

Another approach is to have the victim in town, but unable to convince anyone around them that what is happening is real, and not a delusion of a sick mind. Stalked through a crowd, the victims are still, ultimately, alone, psychologically isolated. They are still helpless.

c. Mounting Tension. There must be a growing sense of tension as the story progresses. There must be suspense, urgency, a building of tension to a climactic confrontation/conclusion. Authors accomplish this by allowing the suspense to build until it seems unbearable, only to release it, temporarily, before building it again and even higher. We've all seen this done in movies, where a person wanders through an empty house, hears a creepy noise, only to have a cat jump out at them. (Those darn cats! They're everywhere.) Then, the tension builds again, with a revived intensity and even greater tension. This creates a sort of cycle of tension; one that builds higher and higher, and ultimately must be resolved.

d. Resolution. By resolution, we mean there must be a climax, some sort of a discharge from the mounting anxiety. **The reader must get liberation from the insupportable tension that has been building throughout the tale**. That's what keeps the reader reading. They want to know how it will all turn out. We've all seen the horror movies where the heroes vanquish the monster (the supposed climax), only to have it suddenly rear up one last time and have to be defeated once more (the true climax). The movie, **Alien**, does it by having the scary monster hiding onboard the life pod. This is a climax in stages. Misdirection is the means to make the audience/reader think it has been resolved when it actually hasn't. Then will come the true resolution. It works well—often.

And there you have it. To recap, for a good science fiction or story to be sci-fi or fantasy with horror in it, it must first be a good story in its own right. It also must need science fiction or fantasy setting as a basic building block(s) to make the whole thing work. Horror has to be an intrinsic part of the plot, not just an overlay. The horror, as well, must also require the science fiction or fantasy aspects in order for it to work. For fantasy, think Lord Of The Rings types of horror. You have the wizard who wants to be all powerful by using the "Dark Arts."

Why is it important that science fiction with horror be just that, and not a horror story with a science fiction overlay? Well, for one thing, many editors do know the difference, as do their readers. They have guidelines. They will reject out of hand any story that isn't true science fiction. They often have strict guidelines in that regard. Many other magazines do this, as well. And, both editors and readers often hate stories that are a mishmash, neither fish nor fowl, and having a weak willing suspension of disbelief as a result. Again, the movie, **Alien**, for example, was scary for a theater audience. But would it work as well for the reader who has more time to pause and question the scenario, the nature of that particular alien, and then their personal willing suspension of disbelief in it? To find that answer, do a little research on your own. The original story the movie was based on is "out there," and it was science fiction. See if you can track it down. If you do; read it. Check out the differences between the written version and the later movie version. That should reveal a lot!

Besides, if you as an author don't know the differences between horror, science fiction, and fantasy, and don't know what constitutes each, and how to write true for each of them, what does that say about you as a writer? Who would want to buy the work of someone who is as slapdash and incompetent, as to put a leprechaun or pixie on a spaceship or a banshee on an alien planet, and doesn't even know the difference? Of course, if you do know the difference and can do it successfully, then you are writing slipstream. But that's a whole 'nother topic!

Basically, horror is where you find it. Whether it is a pathological murderer, as in the movie, **Psycho,** a monster in

Alien, or an evil demon in **Lord Of The Rings**, the horror must mostly conform to the above requirements to work well. Seriously, and if you want to be taken seriously by editors and readers alike, you, as an autho,r must know the different genres, what defines them, and more importantly, how to write horror in them successfully. Failure to do this will probably result in you being a failure as a writer, and/or a host of rejection slips. And that would be a true horror in science fiction, fantasy, or whatever, because we need all the good authors we can get! New blood is essential in any field. Just ask any vampire!

CHAPTER 12

Is Self-Censorship Necessary To Get Published?

"It's a beautiful thing, the destruction of words. "

— *1984*, George Orwell

What can we safely say anymore? What's left to talk about that isn't dangerous to our writing reputations or careers might stop us from getting our science fiction, fantasy, and horror stories published? What topics can we write about without any repercussions to our wallets or ourselves, yet still have something relevant left to say? Such questions loom large on the sci-fi writer's horizon. They loom larger with each passing year, because the situation is getting worse, and quickly.

Like it or not, there is less we can "safely" write about, fewer topics we dare openly explore, delve into, or examine, because we fear a backlash if we do. That's the sad truth. Where science fiction writers once felt free to write about almost anything, now we constrain ourselves. We practice self-censorship and often to a high degree.

What is the reason for this state of affairs? Who is responsible? OURSELVES! You see, censorship comes from without, and there is a tremendous amount of that lately, due in large part, I personally believe, to "Political Correctness," and perhaps, also, the political times in which we live.

Is such censorship warranted? I make no claims to know that answer, because it's a big question, certainly bigger than I am! One could argue that some censorship is good, I suppose. Others would say no, there should be no censorship in a free society. My personal opinion is each of us, as individuals, must make our own decision on that score.

But what I'm talking about here is not a censorship imposed from without, but self-censorship, that which comes from within ourselves, from us, as writers. Can exterior forces, such as being politically correct, cause or contribute to this phenomenon? Oh, yes. Pressure through being "PC" or other powers, such as government, morality groups, etc., can all cause us to be cautious or refrain from writing about certain, now considered "dangerous," topics. I think the list of such dangerous topics is growing annually. And that gives me some cause for worry. Even censorship in a good cause can go too far, and we don't usually realize that until it has already done just that.

If in doubt about this, just think about the McCarthy Era in the United States. This was in the early 1950s, when writers, actors, directors, producers, artists, musicians, and intellectuals of all sorts, all became targets of Senator McCarthy and his fierce, dogmatic, anti-communist campaign. For want of a better term, it was a witch hunt.

Even those who were innocent of any wrongdoing (and this was the vast majority of the people mentioned), ducked and covered, led circumscribed lives, did not associate with former friends or acquaintances that were now "tainted" by McCarthy and his minions' accusations, whether those people were truly guilty or not. Some fled the country, such as the famous actress, Ingrid Bergman, along with many others. Some simply lost their jobs, their careers, and often their marriages and families. Oh well!

And this isn't a one-off problem, either. Repeatedly, and throughout American history, people have suffered such witch hunts, starting with the Salem Witch Trials of our Colonial Period, and continuing, periodically, to today. We, as Americans, seem to do this on a regular basis. It really seems to be a periodic thing with us. But as bad as these witch hunts can be, it is what we do to ourselves, as a result of them that worries me most.

We authors of science fiction, fantasy, and horror, may be performing a slow writing suicide, killing our own genres through fear. Our genres are particularly susceptible to this sort of thing. When we create our "Brave New World," as Aldous Huxley did, we often create societies with unpleasant, negative, or even shocking aspects, ones that may no longer be politically correct, but ones created to show a definite point, to illustrate something we feel needs to be brought to the public's attention. But to avoid negative labels, I think a lot of us now avoid such topics altogether, or water them down until they are worthless, as far as making any real statement goes. It seems, one way or the other, we authors have finally invoked our own version of George Orwell's *Newspeak*.

So, just what is *Newspeak* and why are we invoking it? Well, in George Orwell's haunting book, *1984*, the government decided to rewrite language. Why? Because if they had total control of the language, they believed that people would be completely under their control, as well, automatically, as it were. If one doesn't have the words "freedom" or "liberty" in one's vocabulary, then one can't even think about them, because we think in words. No word for something—no concept of that something—it's gone. It's that simple.

For instance, instead of such basic ideas as "good" and "bad," the speaker of *Newspeak* might only say (and therefore, *think*) "good" and "ungood."

Now what's the difference between "ungood" and "bad?" Well, "bad" has much more of a negative connotation by far. So if one said, "the government is bad," that would be much worse for someone to hear than someone just saying that at times the government was "ungood." The former concept starts riots and rebellions. The latter one merely expresses an almost neutral or casually negative, but mild opinion.

Now again, I'm not saying that some self-censorship isn't warranted, or a "good" thing. Nor am I saying that it is "ungood." But carried to extremes, as I think is happening now, I fear it might become very "ungood."

Edgar Rice Burroughs, for example, and an author I used to read avidly as a kid, is by today's standards, a raging racist. Rudyard Kipling was accused of the same thing, because of his strong belief in "empire," and "the "white man's burden" to civilize. But in Burroughs's own times, the majority of Americans thought much the way he thought. He was not unusual, but just one of a very big crowd. As terrible as that sounds, it was so. So, to those of his own time, those contemporaries he wrote for, he wasn't much of a racist, if at all, by the overall standards of that day.

Now, we can't see him any other way, but racist. It dominates our attitudes toward his work. By today's standards, he's an unmitigated bigot. So I'm betting many of today's parents wouldn't want their children to read Burroughs' books if they knew this. And yet, what a loss that is, in a way, because my imagination soared to magical heights when I read his novels about Mars. I was there, fighting with swords, racing through the thin dying Martian atmosphere—you name it—I was doing it all.

Was Burroughs really a racist? Oh, yes, there is no doubt about that. By today's standards he was. But should we throw the "good" out with the "ungood," or can we, as rational adults, discern what to enjoy and what to reject in his writings? Can we teach our children to do the same? After all, Burroughs did give several generations a wish to explore, a sense of being able to reach for the stars, to have a curiosity about them. And if he was a racist, well then he was also a victim of his times, because pretty much everyone was to some real degree.

And I, as a reader, am I perfectly capable as an individual of rejecting the negative in his stories, but still able to see the wonder? I think so, and I hope most of us can do this. Most lovers of classical music can enjoy Wagner, his operas and such, and this despite his bigoted personal political leanings. The listener of his music can separate that marvelous stuff from the man's dreadful beliefs as a man. So why shouldn't we do the same with Edgar Rice Burroughs, or Rudyard Kipling?

So, I do think as writers of science fiction and authors of other genres as well for that matter, we should all give serious thought as to how much self-censorship we invoke. And beware of *Newspeak*! It can be so dangerous.

The news media these days loves to substitute single letters followed by the word, "word," instead of saying the actual word itself, as in "the F-word," or the "N-word." But if we all do this in our writing, isn't there an inherent danger that if we lose a word like this in our language, we lose the concept of it as well, the very danger that goes and is inherent in such a word, as *Newspeak* would have us do?

If we can't even think the word, remember how we used and invoked it, aren't we in danger of forgetting the atrocities such a word represented? Do we then erase them from our history? And if we do that, aren't we in danger of then repeating such atrocities, because the harsh lessons learned from them will be lost? Do we rewrite *Tom Sawyer* or *Huckleberry Finn*? And if we do, aren't we weakening the very idea of just how bad slavery really was? I don't think that's something we should ever forget.

If a word just becomes "ungood" instead of actually "bad," might we not forget the bad things such words caused? Might they then become just "ungood" instead of "horrible" atrocities? Might it then become easier to repeat those atrocities? I repeat this, because I think it is a very big danger.

Oh, nobody wants to say terrible words. That's a given. And I'm not saying we should use them casually, any time we feel like it, or under any circumstances in our writing. Careful thought always should be given to doing such a thing. But, if we wipe them from our language altogether, we may be in danger of wiping the history, sad, "ungood," or otherwise, that goes with them. And I repeat that this could be dangerous. As "they" say, it might condemn us to repeating history.

Now, even having written this article was a trial for me. I was actually afraid that even the mere subject would evoke too much of a negative response. I did write about this on a blog, and in a chat room, and felt strongly enough about the subject where I thought I should write about it here, as well. But, my intention certainly isn't to offend anyone. It is merely to raise the subject and get us all to thinking about it, because censorship is a subject worth contemplating, isn't it? After all, it does affect what we write, how we can write, and what we should write and to what extent we can write about something.

And, isn't the fact that I just felt I had to explain myself and why I wanted to write about this, indicative of what I'm talking about, a symptom of the whole thing—how far this political correctness has already gone? There is a problem, but even to raise the issue nowadays seems dangerous. It's "ungood." But I do think we should at least consider the topic of self-censorship. I truly am afraid it may be going too far.

And if you doubt this, then let me just wish you a "Happy Holidays," because that's definitely safer to say these days than anything else—well, there is always "Seasons Greetings," too, I suppose.

Am I being silly about this? A little, perhaps, but check this out: have you heard the latest from Down Under, meaning Australia? Our news media on Thanksgiving week, reported that some people want to revise Santa Claus down there! Santa shouldn't say "Ho-Ho-Ho" anymore, apparently! He should now say "Ha-Ha-Ha," because the phrase "ho" has negative connotations in American street slang.

Now do you see what I mean? Isn't this all just going a little too far? Don't let anything "ungood" happen to you! If you are writing science fiction, fantasy, or horror, and have some point, something with regard to political, religious, or social commentary you want to make, then I feel you should make it. Consider carefully how you go about this, though, because if you go too far, no publisher will publish you. So not only what you say, but how you go about saying it is very important here. Be aware of people's sensibilities, and make darn sure that what you have to say is to help point out a problem, or a solution, and not just to further some bigoted belief of your own.

CHAPTER 13

Selling Yourself As An Author—You Can Do It!

So after all this great advice, have you written a truly great story? And now you just bet you're going to be the next J.K. Rowling, because it's such an awesome tale? You're just positive every editor you send it to will have to love it, because how could they possibly not? Right? So, amidst them all wrangling over which one gets the wonderful privilege of publishing your literary masterpiece, you suddenly discover, **TA-DA! YOU'VE ARRIVED!** Right again?

Well, probably—that is—most likely, this is not going to be the case. You see, it just "ain't" that easy to become known as a truly great author. By "great author," I mean here the kind of author whose last name is "Creighton," "King," "Rice," "Rowling," or some such other fabled appellation. Heck, for that matter, I'm even talking about how hard it is to achieve mid- to low-level author status. None of it is easy to attain, not easy at all!

Why is this? Well, I'm sure we've all heard the trite phrase "having to pay one's dues." We all know what it means, that we as "artists have to suffer," blah, blah, yada, yada—and all that cliché stuff. How tiresome to hear it yet again, right? What a bummer! And the mental image this "suffering" thingy usually evokes isn't really so bad, is it? I mean, just picture the ancient, but rather romantic idea of living on the Left Bank in Paris. Imagine little "you" starving in some rundown garret, freezing cold, and having to use some old typewriter (with one bad key, of course) to knock out in a mere three months' time **THE NEXT GREAT NOVEL**! But wonder of wonders, you did it!

Hey, it happened sort of that way for J.K. Rowling, didn't it? So it could happen for you, too? Well, not exactly. First, there are conflicting stories of how Ms. Rowling wrote her first Harry Potter book and under what conditions, but the circumstances definitely weren't that romantic, or nearly so quick. Ah, well, it still makes for a good literary legend. And although legends help us get through our lives, they are not the stuff of life when it comes to actually getting published. Reality, by it's very definition, is the "real" stuff of life, I'm afraid.

So, wake up my little muffins! Smell the bitter coffee. Because "it's a jungle out there," as "they" like to say. Seriously, all joking and kidding aside, it really is a jungle, or worse, and that is what you as an author must face in order to make it "big" or otherwise, if at all.

In this book, you've been given the tools to write a darn good book. If you adhered to what I've said in these pages, then your work will be better than average. However, that is no longer enough just to write a great story. Those days for authors are long over. Writing a marvelous tale, then sitting back and leaving it to editors/publishers to sell your work for you is now history.

I've said it before, but it bears repeating. Now, you aren't just a writer anymore, you have to be a salesman as well, and a darn good one if you want to get published. More, you have to be your own publicist, personal assistant, secretary, editor, proofreader, and whatever else it takes to break into the writing-world-as-we-now-know-it.

Why is it so tough? Well, there are thousands and thousands of would-be authors out there, just like you! With e-submissions now common, anyone, anywhere in the world that wants to submit something can, and they do! This means slush piles are huge and growing all the time. Editors wade through mountains of the stuff and often will only read a paragraph or two before tossing a story or novel to one side and moving onto the next. Remember that opening chapter about the five steps to getting published, and the definite need for a "hook?" This is why. The editor just isn't going to read your whole work, but rather he'll glance at the first few sentences of it only. So you'd better catch them right off with that hook! This bears repeating, because the hook is the only way you are going to get your literary foot in the publisher's door.

Then there is the cost-of-doing-business factor. The expenses of producing books in hard print rise steadily, even as the market for such novels steadily drops. That's so not good! It doesn't look pretty for publishing as a whole and certainly not for you as an aspiring author.

E-publishing is helping—it is growing on an annual basis and that's good news for authors, but there are problems with that as well. Many editors won't proofread your work anymore. If they accept it, they leave it up to you to proof and properly edit it. They don't have the time. And, much less is often charged for people to read your work in an e-book format and this means, of course, less in the way of royalties for you—often much less. E-publishers mostly don't pay advance fees to authors. Usually, you must rely strictly upon the sales themselves. However, the royalty share for you, as an author, is often substantially higher this way than for print books. The only real exception to this seems to be the mainstream print publishers, who want e-book rights that include much smaller royalties to you than many newer e-book publishing houses do.

And there are so many e-publishing houses coming and going these days. For a would-be author, it's a minefield as to which one they should submit a story or novel. "Mom and Pop" e-publishers fail on a regular basis. So pick the wrong e-publisher and you can lose the rights to your novel in bankruptcy proceedings, because it is often considered an "asset" of the publisher's. At the very least, your story may be tied up for months, perhaps even years, before you get the rights to it back again. And whether or not they pay you royalties due you is another minefield altogether. And this has happened to me several times over the years, and I don't consider myself stupid. So if it can happen to me, it can happen to you, too. You really must research these publishers before you sign with them. Google them. Look for complaints about them. Check them out before signing.

Another problem in this area is some e-publishers will publish almost anything. It doesn't cost much for them to do it, and if even a few such novels are sold on a monthly basis, it is extra money in their pocket. They often "pad" their literary stable this way, as it were. This is just business. It's nothing personal. But this also means there are tons of badly written books and/or stories out there. Readers now must swim through a deluge of such books to find good ones, one they'll like. So it makes it that much harder for a good book to stand out in such a crowded field.

So, you say hard print then is the answer? Well, as I've already mentioned, hardcover readership is declining, and has been for years and will continue to do so. This is a long-term trend, my little cookies. It is going to continue for some time to come, I fear. That's reality again.

So here you are, an authorial voice crying in a vast wilderness of writers and a sea of poor quality books. You are unheard, unloved, and so unpaid. What can you do about it? Well, here is an approach that seems to work.

1. First, practice your art of writing. Follow the steps in the first chapter carefully. **Make sure you truly have written something worthwhile**. Then,

2. Research the publishers who might publish your work. Just because they publish science fiction, doesn't mean they publish your style of science fiction. Some prefer dark; some prefer technical/hard SF. Some prefer young adult. Some want Mundane; others want space opera, etc. Horror and Fantasy are the same way. Some publishers definitely don't want sword and sorcery fantasies anymore. Many horror publishers are fed up with vampires and werewolves. But others still want these.

So dig into it. Make sure you are targeting the right publishers with your work. That's a must. If they want a query letter, look up on the Internet as to how to write a good one. It's amazing how such well-written letters can work and work well. The movie **Alien** is said to have been sold as "Jaws in space." The original **Star Trek** series was said to have been promoted to television executives as "a Wagon Train in space." (It seems westerns were big at the time, I guess, so somehow you have to relate to them.) If this is true, then your query letter should incorporate this sort of thing. In order to get published, **you first must sell your work to the editor/publisher.** See? So already you're a salesman, as well as a writer.

3. It doesn't stop there, as I've already said. Now the real job begins. You may have sold your work to an editor, but now you have to pitch in and help sell it to the readers. **You must market your work!** Self promotion is key. **Did you know many editors will "Google" you to find out what you've done and who you really are?** I had one editor admit to doing exactly that before accepting my story. So it isn't enough to just send them your resume; they want to know more, as in how big a name you really are, what your track record is. Many links to you often seems to equal lots of popularity in an editor's eyes. At the very least, they want to see how and if you are promoting your own work.

4. You must market yourself, as well as your work. Editors Google to not only see who you are and what you've done, but they do it to see if you are marketing yourself, as well as you work. There are many ways of going about this.

Firstly, it is imperative you have your own webpage. That's an absolute must nowadays. You can also attend conventions, hand out personalized bookmarks, flyers, etc., all promoting yourself. Do book signings. Get business cards and hand them out. Even buying books and selling them to bookshops yourself is something many authors now do. Reviews of your novel/story help. The more and the better they are, the better for you as an author. They generate more links for you if online. So you may want to send out or inquire of many reviewers and review sites on the Internet if they will review your work. Some authors have their book covers designed and paid for by themselves. This is to control the first thing the reader sees, the cover. (You'd be surprised how important that can be.) And books must have covers, even if you make them yourself. No cover is a big "no-no" these days.

Having interviews done is another good way to go. Getting yourself on podcasts is another. Some writers do lectures at schools, libraries, anywhere they can. Some charge for this. Others do it free. There are many ways to market yourself. Some ways will work better than others will for you.

I'm into book trailers now. It creates links to my name on the Internet, and more importantly, to my work. It does this quickly and very cheaply, exposes not only me, but my writing to lots of possible readers. Give it a shot. For me, conventions are fun, but I don't think they are truly very helpful, unless they are the bigger ones. However, being on panels helps. Other members of panels are usually other authors and—yes—editors and publishers, as well! It doesn't hurt to network with them.

5. Announce yourself. Let everyone know you are an author! Sign all your letters, emails, etc. with your name as being an author. Include your website address, email address, blogs, and/or book trailer sites below your signature. Get it in there. You can even add short blurbs about a new novel or story about to be published. And do blogs! Get your face and name out there. Do book reviews, if you want. You'll learn quickly this way, what makes for a popular and good book versus a bad one, believe me! Do a newsletter, online or off; they help to announce who you are, what you are doing, what is available from you, etc.

Do you see what I mean? You are no longer just a writer. You have to be a publicist, your own personal assistant, you name it, and you have to be it. Editors not only expect this these days, but many demand it. They see you as a partner in the business of publishing their/your work. So you had better decide right now that you are going to be that partner. And, although you may not romantically starve in a Parisian garret while writing a marvellous tome, you will work your tail off I'm telling you!

Is it a tough world out there for authors? Oh, yeah! The publishing world has chewed up many a promising author and spit them out, and often over trivial things. **SO PROCEED INTO THE PUBLISHING WORLD WITH CAUTION! It's a dangerous place for "newbies," and even "oldbies."**

However, if you do most of what I'm advising here, and if your stories are actually good ones, you'll start to rise in the publishing world. When I first started, I wrote for the lowest paying magazines, anyone actually, that was kind and generous enough to publish me. That got my name out there. Now, I'm being published in so-called "pro" markets, but it is the low paying markets I owe my sincere thanks to. They are the ones who were willing to take a chance on me in the first place. And remember, just because they were low paying doesn't mean they had less to lose. Being smaller publishers, for them that "low pay" was still a lot of money to come up with, proportionately speaking.

Am I at the top of my profession? **I WISH!** But I'm climbing steadily, making headway each month and each year. You can, too. My work is being sold more often and for more money. You can have that, too. Be positive! Be persistent and persevering, and above all, work at it! Get off your butt and take an active role in marketing your own work and yourself.

It's not just "publish or perish" anymore. Now it's "publish and promote or perish." You can do it, my little minions. I have faith in you. I want to see you all climbing up that ladder behind me (I'll ignore those higher than me on it for now), but remember, if you get too close to me—I kick! Hey, it's an author-eat-author world out there. Seriously though, stick to it, and you'll get there. That's a promise. Now, if I can just watch out for those above me on the literary ladder trying to kick me off! Hey, you! Yeah, you! Get out of my way! I'm coming up through! I'm climbing to the top. And so can you!

CHAPTER 14

Self-Publishing—A Viable Alternative?
You Betcha!

Self-publishing. For me, that has always equated to those detestable two words: **VANITY PRESS!** And I've always shunned those like the plague. They usually produced inferior books, had little or no distribution, and/or the books themselves were so expensive, nobody would buy them. They were really just to assuage the author's vanity, in my opinion, hence the moniker, Vanity Press. Admittedly, some are better than others, have come a long way, but having checked them out, they still aren't near what I want or need in the way of a publishing alternative for myself.

However, we are living in times when e-book sales are multiplying, even as print books sales are falling, and over a long term, as mentioned in the prior chapter. However, print books still are the biggest part of the publishing market by far and will be for some time to come, no doubt. So, either we place our books with an online e-publisher, or try really hard to go through print publishers (and often not succeed). We have few other options to this. Vanity Press is a poor one of them, in my personal opinion.

And now there is another problem these days; publishers, both e-book and print, seem more intent on marketing themselves, rather than their authors. Oh, not all of them, and not the big, mainstream, print ones, so much, but the handwriting does seem to be on the wall there in this regard. As their profits fall, the available money for marketing authors shrinks. So out of necessity, and more and more, authors are being pressured to do this for themselves. Let's be honest; if you're a publisher and you have only so much marketing money, you are going to spend most of it on the most likely authors, the ones that sell the best, and also on your own company to keep its name out there. So bye-bye, little or not well-known authors. It's already this way. If you are Stephen King or J.K. Rowling, you get the lion's share of marketing money. If you are an unknown professor; good luck!

But now there is a new, and I feel true, self-publishing system coming online, literally, and figuratively. **Smashwords** is one of the best examples of this. This site allows you to self-publish your books. They guide you step-by-step in the upload of your work; have an automated system for formatting conversions of it to all the major types of e-book formats, assign you separate pages for each of your books, plus a profile page for yourself. They have direct links to graphs and charts (continuously updated) of your sales. They even assign ISBN numbers to your books and for free! All you have to do is write the stories, and create your own cover (and that last is optional). Plus, they have a marvelous distributorship/affiliate program. Your books go to such places as Sony, Apple, Kobo—well, almost everywhere, it seems like. And they have their own vast site which promotes and distributes your works, too.

How much does all this cost? Well, surprisingly, it's **FREE!** Yep, I'm using the magic word, one often much maligned by liars and thieves in the marketing world, but in this case, it's actually valid. **Smashwords** is free. Even the ISBN number, if you name **Smashwords** as the publisher, is free! No charge, nothing, nada! You get the lion's share of the royalties, way above what almost any e-publisher is willing to give you, you get to track your sales, so there is no funny business, and with an automated system that helps ensure this. You are emailed (if you like) for every sale and/or review of your book. And, you can upload short stories, novels, novellas, and anthologies, whatever. They just have to be complete works.

Am I receiving a kickback for this marvelous review of their site? Nope—nothing! I'm just so enthused with it that I had to share this with my fellow struggling authors. Here, at long last, is an outlet for self-publishing that is professional, with widespread distribution, and all sorts of other goodies and it's all free! Now, the affiliates demand a percentage of every sale, as they always do, of course, so your sales from the **Smashwords** site give you higher royalties. They also have site-wide promotions, discount coupons you can email to favorite fans, sales, etc. But even the distributors' take is not high, so again, the author receives the lion's share of all royalties, far more than practically any e-book or print publisher will give you, or could afford to give you!

Do you still have to market? You bet. That's a sign of the times, but **Smashwords** also makes available a marketing plan book for free, as well as allowing links to actual print sites for your story, and/or podcasts, as well. See what I mean? This is true self publishing in my opinion, and again, it's **FREE!**

CreateSpace is another marvelous site if you want your books in actual print. They actually have a distributorship, as well, and the prices are low and quality of their print books is high. You get quite a choice as to what size book you want, too. What's more, this is all free as well! And, they have a free program that allows you to create covers for your books. You do not have to order a minimum number of books to do this. Again, to have your books available in print is free. When you do order books, you will find they are certainly cheap enough to resell them and still make a tidy profit, if that's what you want to do.

But my opinion is that for book signings, I'll do that, but otherwise, I won't. I just want them available to readers in print who want to order them through either CreateSpace or a distributor outlet. Another thing, your books will be available worldwide if you choose to opt for their expanded distribution system at a nominal fee. Again, this is not vanity press in my opinion, but true self-publishing. Instead of paying hundreds, even thousands of dollars, you can actually make your books available in print for free.

Amazon.com owns **CreateSpace**, but it also allows you to publish your books for free in Kindle format. Again, like the other two outlets, it allows you to track your sales yourself, set your own prices, etc. And also, just as with the other two, it's entirely free! Oh, with all of them you can pay to have the work done for you, but if you are willing to do it yourself (following all of their easy guidelines), there is absolutely no charge to have your books available at all three of these sites. And **Amazon.com** also is set up so that your books are available in Kindle format around the world. They have **Amazon.co.uk** (for Great Britain), as well as in Germany, and so many other places.

Between these three sites alone, your books can be sent to a multitude of e-book distributors (including Barnes & Noble and so many others), as well as in print and so readily available at many print outlets, even around the world. There are other sites like **Smashwords, Amazon.com** and **CreateSpace** coming on line, so do yourself a favor and check them out, as well! Select the one(s) you think are right for you, but for me, it's **Smashwords, Amazon.com,** and **CreateSpace**.

Again, I get nothing out of this from these sites, nor do I want to. What I wanted to do was share with my fellow authors a new way of self-publishing, and for free. I don't know about you, but again, I have darn little money to spend on marketing, so this to me was a big boon! And, I'm making sales. So, do yourself a favor, and at least check these sites out. **Smashwords**, to my way of thinking, is absolutely wonderful, especially for e-books, as is **Amazon.com** for Kindle, and **CreateSpace** for print.

Self-publishing, the real thing seems to be here at long last, and it's affordable, if "free" isn't too high a price! So check it out! Again, it's getting to be strictly up to us authors to do the work, so roll up those sleeves and just do it!

CHAPTER 15

A Matter of Faith—Religion in SF, Fantasy, And Horror

The title of this article may seem like an oxymoron, a contradiction in terms. To some writers, it definitely is. For them, religion has no place at all in science fiction, fantasy, or horror writing, but this is especially so for the genre of hard science fiction. The very idea of it is anathema to such authors. Science and religion, in their view, are incompatible subjects, best kept apart; separate, like issues of church and state. They want only hard evidence, not faith. They usually refer to this sort of definition of faith:

> "**1.** Confident **belief** in the truth, value, or trustworthiness of a person, idea, or thing.
>
> **2. <u>Belief that does not rest on logical proof or material evidence</u>.**" [Emphasis added.]
>
> **— The Free Dictionary.com**

So, if something is based on a "belief," as both definitions use the term, rather than a hard scientific fact, they want nothing to do with it. Neither do many fantasy writers, at least not in the sense of it being a real issue. They often prefer, instead, to create mythological religions, ones that group around made-up gods of their own choosing. Horror stories do sometimes deal with religion, and these may even involve attacks of some sort or another on established churches. But overall, even in this last genre, authors tend to avoid the issue of faith more often than not. It's just too "touchy" a subject for them, "too hot to handle," it seems.

Still, to some writers of these genres, it is a valid issue and one they wish to write about in depth. I agree with these authors. This is not because of my personal religious convictions, which are my own concern. Rather, in my view, it is because if science fiction, fantasy, and horror wish to be taken seriously, then these genres must exercise an innate curiosity about everything in the multiverse. It must discuss and question it all, even questions regarding religion and if (or if not) there is a Creator/God. In other words, virtually no subject should be taboo to the writer, although, I do "believe" in the exercise of good taste and good judgment whenever possible.

Besides, there are always those fussy editors to contend with, and writing on unsavory subjects may result in the writer not being published. Publishers, then, in response to the pressure of the clamoring public's tastes, are the strongest and surest form of censors in this regard. Publishers have to be, to survive in the business, to make money. Yet, I think they are enough of a censoring device. In my personal opinion, I don't think we writers need any more on top of that.

My first real taste of religion in science fiction came from the author, Arthur C. Clarke. As a child, I read an old anthology of his, which included a short story entitled, *The Star*, which was about a Jesuit priest/astrophysicist on an exploratory trip to a sun that had gone supernova long ago. Far out on the fringes of that blasted solar system, they found a repository of a destroyed race's very humanlike accomplishments, including their music, art, and the sciences. They seemed a wonderful people. It turned out (quite dramatically, I thought), that this supernova was the Star of Bethlehem. It caused the priest to question his God as to why a race had to be put to the supernova "sword" so that their sun could light the way for his own faith's savior. It deeply affected his beliefs on his place in the order of things.

Compelling stuff, huh? And Clarke has written many other works concerning God and religion. His classic short story, *The Nine Billion Names of God*, is one more example. The conclusion, with humanity's mission accomplished by having used computers to speed up finding all possible names for God, ends with the stars blinking out one-by-one, the universe ending. His novel, *Childhood's End*, is yet another such excursion into the subject. His aliens, who were actually quite civilized and nice, looked very much like the devil, and their task was to serve a godlike super being, whose aims were to transmute the human race to its needs, through the children, and thus ending the human race, as we know it. Perhaps Clarke could be less than subtle on such issues at times (downright blatant on occasion), but his stories always carried a lot of meaning. They had a lot to say.

Nor is Arthur C. Clarke alone on using religion in his stories. Countless famous and not-so-famous authors have as well. Robert Heinlein's, *Job: A Divine Comedy*, is an example. Douglas Adams, of *A Hitchhiker's Guide to the Galaxy* fame, touches on the subject in a number of his novels. Frank Herbert's, *Dune Messiah*, as well as his other *Dune* books, certainly delves into the matter. In horror stories, there are countless examples of this, as well, as in *The Omen, Revelation,* and such. Numerous works question, discuss, or comment on various religions, the nature of God versus Humankind, and a host of such related subjects. The novel by Dan Brown, *The Da Vinci Code,* is an example of this last. And then, with regard to fantasies, we have so many works where the "the beast" is embodied in some for or other, where evil is incarnate as some monstrous entity that must be challenged. So all the genres do deal with this, at least, to some degree.

Now, I do have a personal preference about such works. For me, it is far more important to watch the main character(s) in the plot, to see how they develop, respond, and/or change due to whatever they discover in the way of answers to fundamental, religious-like questions. The Jesuit priest in *The Star*, abused by the notion of God killing an entire alien race so that light could shine upon Bethlehem, was riveting stuff. Again, the priest's responses, his personal inner torment and turmoil, are what caught my attention and held me fast.

When a science fiction, fantasy, or horror story crosses over into what I would call proselytizing, or a not-so-subtle attempt to convert me, as the reader to some belief, then my warning flags go up immediately. It's not that their authors don't have the right to write such things, and not that there aren't outlets for such works. And that's fine. I even wrote a story that was published in such a venue. But there, the reader knows in advance what type of stories he will be reading. The fact that they are pro-religious and mostly Christian-oriented is not unknown, or unexpected by the potential reader. That's as it should be.

My problem is when a writer disguises a personal religious tract as science fiction, fantasy, or horror, and then pounds the pulpit on some ism or other. Is it wrong or just "not good" to do this? No. As writers, more than most others, we should realize the value of free speech, literary openness, the right to write what we want, and have tolerance for all other authors who do.

But I do think it usually makes for a bad story or novel. When the whole point of the thing is to expound on some ism or other to the detriment of any plot, then I'm betting the story is going to be dull. It's usually slow, possibly quite boring, or at least tedious, and with few exceptions. Also, not all readers, by any means, are of one faith or necessarily adherents to any faith at all. So a strenuous conversion effort masquerading as a sci-fi or horror story probably won't be at all well received. Many would find it offensive. Again, in my opinion, whether they write such things or not is solely up to the individual author. But good luck on getting it published when you do!

So should we write about religion, even (if we dare) in hard science fiction? Yes, I think we should. No doors should remain closed. No subjects should be off limits to any author. Just keep in mind that your story, whatever the nature of it, or the subject, should first be a story! Make it good. Show us the characters struggling, changing, and developing. Give us insight into them. Don't make your story a stiff dissertation on why one faith or faction is more important than another is, but instead make it a story that the reader will want to read, and will like for its own sake. So whether a horror story like *The Exorcist* (book or movie version), a fantasy like *The Witch, The Lion, And The Wardrobe*, or something by Arthur C. Clarke, you should include religion if it is important for you to do so.

So, whether your plot is about Shiva, God, Buddha, Confucius, or anything else of a religious nature, **primarily remember what you are; that is, a storyteller. Be proud of that!** We are an old and venerable profession. We date back much farther than the classics, with Homer and his *Iliad* or *Odyssey*—those stories about gods and goddesses of ancient Greece. We sat around cave dwellers' campfires regaling our tribes. We storytellers predate the rise of Christianity, Islam, Judaism, and a host of other religions. We have always been there. Hopefully, we always will be there, to tell a good story. That's our job, so see that you do it! "Believe" in it, even if you believe in nothing else.

CHAPTER 16

Science Fiction's Future—Is It A Mundane One?

Have you checked out one of the relatively new faces of science fiction these days? It's called "mundane." This subgenre is getting quite popular. In fact, as I write this, there is a contest currently running with a science fiction magazine for authors to write a short sci-fi story in this "mundane" style. I suppose this was inevitable. With the rapid advances in the sciences, and the now constant struggle science fiction has just in order to offer fiction before science turns it into fact (as discussed by me in a prior chapter here at AlienSkin Magazine), this probably would have to happen. Still, it took me somewhat by surprise. I just wasn't prepared for how rapidly the face of science fiction is changing. I didn't realize how many more editors are demanding science fiction that is now more fact than fiction.

Oh, and in case you haven't noticed, this chapter deals specifically with science fiction, and not fantasy, or horror, because this topic applies only to science fiction, really.

Now, just what do I mean by mundane? Well, often we are seeing guidelines for stories/novels which must be set in the near future, and the stories must be of a "realistic" future (otherwise referred to as "mundane"), as those guidelines so state. The word, mundane, according to Mirriam-Webster's Online Dictionary, means:

> *"1: of, relating, or characteristic of the world*
>
> *2: characterized by the* **practical,** *transitory, and* **ordinary***:* **commonplace,** *the* **mundane** *concerns of* **day-to-day life.***"*
> [Emphasis and underscores added.]

So by that definition, editors usually mean that you can't have stories about UFOs, transcendental aliens, or even aliens at all. They want stories about futures where just the logical progression of what *now exists* can be extrapolated forward by a few decades. In other words, if we don't have true nanotechnology now, they don't want stories about fantastic changes due to future nanotechnology. If we don't have faster-than-light space travel now, they don't want novels about those either. What they do want is, again, "realistic" stories about the near-term future, such as interplanetary space travel within our own solar system, moon bases, overpopulation, results of further global warming, rising sea levels – that sort of thing. So, out go alien contact stories, interstellar empires, future earths almost magically transformed by strange, new, and wonderful technologies and instead, we can have cloning, coastal flooding, overcrowding, and food shortages.

My first reaction to this sort of thing is to cry out in a loud clear voice, **IT'S BEEN DONE! AND MANY TIMES BEFORE!** I mean, I've read countless stories for decades now about a drowned New York City, people eating **Soylent Green** crackers for meals, wars over diminishing resources, etc., etc. There just have been so many such tales already written, so many novels covering these concepts in depth, and repeatedly, that I'm bored with them now.

But then reason asserted itself (or what passes for reason in my specific case), and my second reaction was to realize that there is always room for new plot twists, new approaches to old themes, and such. So considering that aspect, why should I be so negative about the growth of "mundane" science fiction? After all, even if you can't do a **Planet of the Apes**, story by such a definition, (because at present, we don't have intelligent apes, supposedly, so we can't have them in the future), you can still do a nuclear holocaust/aftermath tale. Of course, I've read countless versions over the years of those, too. Andre Norton was a master at them, although, considering some of the more exotic aspects of her stories (true telepathy; for instance), they couldn't be classified as "mundane," as we know it now.

But authors are flexible. They do have a way of approaching such plots with new twists, new ideas, and novel outcomes. So, more power to them if they can still manage it. At the very least, one could consider writing such a "mundane" tale a challenge worthy of the attempt.

Still, why is there this growing interest in mundane science fiction? For what reason(s) do editors seem to want more stories about a "realistic" near-term future, instead of some far-flung, wonderful imagining? Well, first, we have to be careful here, because some will now shout at me that "mundane" is just a synonym for "hard" science fiction and so has always been around. In fact, this is not the case. "Mundane" is not the same thing as classic hard science fiction, but rather is a more specific subgenre of it, if anything.

Hard science fiction allowed for interstellar empires, for example, if only by means of "slow" ship trade routes and such. Hard science fiction allowed for alien contact, since it is quite reasonable to assume there could be other intelligent species. And hard science fiction allowed for the possibility of fantastic futures, given the laws of physics, possibility of wormholes, white holes, even the idea of parallel universes (M-Brane theory), and all. Why, even time travel just might squeak in under the guidelines for hard science fiction, because some physicists say it may be possible, and some are actually working on realizing such a thing in a practical way right now. Of course, that one may be a *little* questionable...

However, with "mundane" science fiction (if one can really even call it science fiction anymore), it would seem to be a natural outgrowth of the rate of current scientific advance. Such advances are coming so quickly, so frequently, that fiction has a hard time staying ahead of fact. For instance, one can hardly talk about Edgar Rice Burroughs's Mars in any realistic sense today. We know too much about Mars now, and the solar system, to pretend there could be Martian maidens, or Venusian flying men, for that matter. Science and its relentlessly encroaching reality has dispelled such notions, bulldozed such romanticized visions of our neighboring worlds to the wayside. Our neighboring planets are now much more prosaic in nature, much more "mundane" in physical reality. Although still extraordinary, in my opinion, the chances of finding advanced life, let alone intelligent life on any of our sister worlds seems small, indeed, these days.

End result—well, editors seem to have given in to some degree and accepted that science fiction should just be an extrapolation of what exists now, rather than wild flights of fancy. They've surrendered to what they think is inevitable, if you will. Science fiction would then just be a short-term projection of current "accepted" science "facts."

So if that's the case, what's left to write about them? Well, it now would appear to be action and/or adventure stories about space jockeys, asteroid miners, and various disputes of territorial rights on the moon. Tales could be about delta-V fuel problems, shifting power plays on an overcrowded, resource-starved Earth and such-like plots of interplanetary intrigue. And of course, there are always the topics of corporate greed, and humanity's attempt to colonize our own system. Toss in cloning, and some nanotechnology and you get a good idea of what is acceptable in Mundane Science Fiction.

Now, are these fertile grounds for plots? Sure they are. They have been in the past often enough. As I've said, if they are approached right and by the right author, they can be made fresh and new. As a line from an episode of the old **Twilight Zone** once said, "There's always room for one more, honey!" Of course, that same statement referred to an available seat on an airplane that blew up in the sky several moments later. Hmm...

And that's what I fear here. Are we embracing reality, the "mundane" world, as the future for science fiction, only to see it blow up in our faces? Do we see science fiction now as just scenarios for near-term and highly probable events instead of possible events? Is science fiction's future only to serve as examples of likely probabilities, probable near-term outcomes?

It would seem, for better or worse, that sci-fi is headed in that direction. Instead of science fiction imagining something new, like energy beings that eat light, for instance, and running with it; "mundane" science fiction wants us to take something that already exists, such as cloning, and then tell us what it might bring in ten years time. (YAWN!)

I don't really understand why this is now so popular. After all, if all these marvelous scientific achievements are coming so thick and fast, don't they show the incredible possibilities of things to come, how very unexpectedly things may turn out? Might not our future be even more fantastic, more incredible, than authors ever conceived of as possible up until now? So shouldn't we as authors venture even farther into even more exotic realms as writers, and not less? Why can't we continue to write about the wildly impossible, instead of just the merely probable or near-term likely outcomes? Who knows? Once we imagine it, some scientist might just make it possible. It's happened before and many times! But first, somebody has to imagine it to begin with, and that's our job as science fiction writers.

I can't help seeing the progenitors and promoters of "mundane" science fiction as wonder thieves, to a certain extent. Where science seems to be opening up magnificent vistas of strange new worlds, these aficionados of the "mundane" seem to be trying to lead us into, and I quote Merriam-Webster's Dictionary here, into writing about the merely "practical," the dreary "ordinary," and the dull "commonplace" world. Is that what science fiction is supposed to be all about? Personally, I don't think so. I read it to enjoy flights of fancy, to soar to heights and places I can't reach by my boring car, or a dreary local New York subway! Only sci-fi authors can take me where I want to go.

Is there a place for such mundane writing in sci-fi literature? Of course, because there should be a place for all writers in our genre and all its subgenres, if they are willing to use their imaginations in any way, shape, or form at all. That, for me, is what science fiction is all about—to explore, to question, to imagine, and most of all to stretch our horizons.

But it can't stop with the merely mundane, the practical, and the commonplace. We should not give up our rich genre heritage of writing strange tales of intergalactic empires, stories of interactions between humans and aliens, plots about life in various forms, organic and/or inorganic, or stories about bizarre planets and strange universes. We should not stop spinning yarns of vast interstellar wars and forerunner civilizations, ones to whom we may owe much. These topics are the very stuff of science fiction. Tales such as these serve to expand the human imagination. They act to display possibilities of what we can do, may think about, perhaps even possibly create some day, and so make real.

After all, where stands a building today, once stood a person on an empty lot with just an idea of what he might build there. Where some writer of old, such as Jules Verne, wrote pure science fiction about a trip to the moon, now we have gone there and beyond. And that for me is one of the primary responsibilities of science fiction authors—not just to tell a good tale, but also to encourage, promote, and elucidate ideas, to show the realm of the improbable as possible.

We are the authors of imagination, not the archivists of the mundane! We are the creators of ideas, not the keepers of the practical! We are the spinners of strange dreams, not mere government-run think tanks! And I, for one, do not want to see the wonder thieves steal that from us as writers.

Again, is there room for the "mundane" in science fiction? Most assuredly. There always has been. But also and more importantly, and foremost in my opinion, there is and should continue to be room for the marvelous in science fiction. For a child or adult alike, not to be able to stare at the stars in a night sky, not to be able to marvel at them and the universe beyond, not to be able to imagine unlikely and wonderful things about them, would be a terrible thing. I often gaze at those same stars and wonder, and I would not want the wonder thieves to take that from me or anyone else!

There are changes in the science fiction genre and that probably is as it should be. Change is a fact. More than that, it's a necessity for our genre to keep evolving, to adapt to each new generation, to remain relevant in an ever-changing world. Still, I would hate our science fiction genre to literally evolve itself out of existence altogether. Leave the think tanks to do their task, to prognosticate near-term problems and solutions to them, and leave us wordsmiths to do our work. After all, it would be a poor life with no wonder left in it, wouldn't it. We may live in a "mundane" and "practical" world, even a "commonplace" one, but we can at least dream strange dreams that go beyond this world, can't we? Or can we? I wonder what the "practical" answer to that question might be.

CHAPTER 17

Faster Than Light Travel—You Can't Get There From Here

Speed; you need it! It is essential for going into space. That is, if you want to really travel "out there." And I'm not talking about drugs here. Well, a little caffeine maybe, to help on those longer trips. But seriously, the logistics of our universe, the incredible distances involved, make fast travel a necessity in order for you to get "there" from "here" in the length of time allowed for in most stories or novels of science fiction, or science fiction horror. Getting around over vast distances just isn't easy or quick.

How great are those distances? They are vast beyond comprehension. As an example, Voyager I, the spacecraft, has been traveling for some twenty-six years; currently, it is ninety times farther out from our sun than the Earth is. That may seem a long ways, because it is. But it also means that Voyager is only just now leaving our own solar system, passing through the "termination shock" area of it. And Voyager's traveling fast, very fast.

And yet all that distance is nothing compared with the distances to the nearest stars. To get to Alpha Centauri, even by traveling at the speed of light (186,000 miles per second, approximately, and impossible to do), would take you over eight years of travel time to get there and come back. That doesn't leave much time left for sightseeing, let alone science fiction plots, does it?

Since sci-fi and sci-fi horror writers know most of this stuff already, I won't belabor the point. (I know—too late, too late!) Just remember, we have a real problem here with commute times to the nearest stars, let alone those much farther away. So, other than using slow generational ships, which are so dreadfully prone to nasty mutinies, messy revolts, and such (and so perhaps great for horror story settings), how do we get our people where we want them and then back before civilization-as-we-know-it ends on Earth? Faster-Than-Light travel, or FTL as it is commonly referred to, is the only way.

In the real world, we haven't come up with it yet. But in science fiction, ships jump in and out of hyperspace, warp space-time, fold it, navigate wormholes, plunge into black holes (not my idea of a good time), travel through earlier versions of our own universe (when distances were shorter but, alas, the universe was much hotter), slip through star gates, resonate into new locations, travel via other dimensions, teleport, invoke quantum drives, etc. Now, what's wrong with all these means? Well, other than the fact that we don't know if they can really exist or work—nothing. They are perfectly legitimate methods for writers of science fiction and horror to employ. Even with these methods, trips can be long. For an example of this, think of the movie, **Alien.** Despite FTL ability, that freighter was still on a long trip!

Is the type of FTL you pick important? It depends. If your plot revolves around the hyper drive, as in something going awry with it, then you need to pay a lot of attention to detail. If, however, your means of travel is strictly secondary to the story, you don't have to dwell on it. Just mention it in passing, as in, "Yeah, yeah, I hopped a space warp freighter to get here. Hey! Who hasn't?" Get it? Don't beat the subject to death. Mention it, make it sound plausible, and then get on with your plot. After all, millions of people drive cars every day. How many of them could explain solid-state ignition systems? I know at least one that couldn't—me. Same for refrigerators; what keeps them cold, tiny little snowmen? But I digress. But my point is that the reader doesn't have to know the "ins and outs" of the method you use in your novel to circumvent the speed of light. They just have to know it works. Again, this is so, but only if the plot doesn't hinge heavily on how the drive works.

But some novels do depend heavily on the type of FTL drive used. This is because it's unlikely that you can have a cohesive interstellar civilization without FTL travel. Interstellar empires could hardly exist in its absence. All your enemies in a revolt would be long dead of old age, as would their descendants be, if you relied on slow ships (below light speed) as a means of quelling uprisings in some distant star colony.

And yes, folks; that same old maxim, *willing suspension of disbelief*, is still at work here. Nobody, except for a very few (and pity those few) would believe a story about an interstellar liner using a squirrel-powered drive. Nuts to that! You've got to come up with something better, something "believable" to the reader. So for your FTL drive, do the following:

1. Give it an interesting name. "Hyper" is kind of old hat. So is "warp." Be more imaginative. I used "Interstitial Drive" in one of my stories, *Without Omens*, as just an example.

2. Describe (briefly) how the FTL drive works. Again, be imaginative. How about using a "Flicker" drive, where ships "flick" in and out of reality? It's really just a version of the "jump" drive, but I make the jumps so tiny that the ships (if the human eye could see it), seem to flicker through space. Don't like that one? Okay. Or again, how about my Interstitial or I-drive? This is based on my idea that the universe might have an underlying sub-matrix (like points on a grid) with space-time nodes. My "I-drive" works by letting ships travel via these nodes. Luckily, it results in FTL travel. Why? Because I made it that way—that's why! And that's what you, as the author, have to do, as well. Find a means of moving people over vast distances in real time. Otherwise, you will have the slowest plots in history, science fiction, or horror-wise.

3. Be internally consistent. No, I don't mean by this you should have your characters eating, drinking, or doing the same things repeatedly. I do mean that once you establish the type of FTL drive you want, and the theory behind it, then don't deviate from it. If it takes wormholes to travel, then make sure you have wormholes where you need them, or your drive can create them as needed..

Now, do you absolutely have to use FTL travel? No. If your intent is to write about what happens on a long (very long) voyage, then by all means, use a "slow" or "generation" ship (slower than light speed) method of travel. That gives you lots (lots and lots) of time to develop you plot while the vessel moves slowly (very slowly) from point "A" to point "B." Some of these types of stories can be riveting. (Yawn!) I'm kidding. Certain stories, again especially science fiction horror stories, lend themselves well to this way of traveling. Think of the movie, **Pandorum**, for instance. But otherwise, for the story to progress, you'll probably want to travel more quickly.

So FTL is important. It speeds up not only your characters' travel time, but the plot as well. So, use faster than light travel and you're story will be as fit as a "FTL." (That's pronounced as in "fiddle" in this case. Get it?) . But just remember, how and how fast your people can move, depends upon their method of travel. And if you want them to get to other stars and in a hurry, than FTL is the only way to go, but even so, you must still make it as believable as possible. Oh, and remember this, as well; for many hard science fiction publishers, FTL is just unacceptable, because current science seems to say it's impossible. I disagree with this. For me, current science seems to have some loopholes in this regard, and as long as they exist, I think writers have a perfect right to exploit them.

CHAPTER 18

Armageddon—Use It In SF, Horror, And Fantasy

"It's the end of civilization as we know it!" If I've heard that once, I've heard it a thousand times. My grandfather said it when the music band, the Beatles, first came to America. My father said it when the Beatles broke up. (Ironic, isn't it?) I said it when I had to sit through a Paul McCartney concert with my father who was acting like some demented 1960's teenager. Whew! Was that ever embarrassing!

I guess what we view as the end of civilization is rather dependent on what we think of as civilization in the first place. And that's my point here. Even people living at the same time, in the same city, can have very differing views on the subject. Don't believe me? Then just ask a very conservative person what they think of the state of our society, and then ask the same question of a left-wing liberal. The answers you get will make you wonder if they are from the same universe, let alone the same city! Oh, they'll both probably agree the world is teetering on the edge of disaster, but the reasons for it being this way will differ vastly between them!

Decadence and dissolution, or renaissance and resurgence, seems to be, largely, in the eye of the beholder. Often that eye is jaundiced. What it "sees" is colored by personal belief systems. It is filtered by preexisting prejudices. In other words, it can largely depend on a person's viewpoint, as to whether civilization is dying or progressing. And that's without a catastrophic occurrence! Imagine what it would be like with Armageddon. But writing about the aftermath of such is just so great for science fiction, horror, or fantasy readers. Much of Andre Norton's stuff was post-apocalyptic, and often had strong elements of fantasy. And I can't think of how many plague-zombie horror stories are out there!

But remember, these are all written from different authors' viewpoints. And that, my fellow writers, is what you need to remember when you are writing end-of-the-world stories: Viewpoint! By this, I do not mean the writer's viewpoint as in omniscient or first person. Instead, I'm talking about how the characters themselves view what is happening. Specifically, what are their feelings, hopes, and aspirations? How do they face their trials, challenges, and their fears? This, then, is the all-important issue. Whatever the catastrophe is, it is just a framework. The characters, and what they go through, are of paramount importance. This is the stuff of life and a good story.

Although the type of Armageddon that characters face is important, and has to be interesting and realistic, it is the characters responses that carry the day. After all, one can write a one-sentence story about the end of the world: "The comet came from space, smashed into the ocean, and wiped out all life on Earth." See? Not very interesting, is it?

So to make it intriguing, there has to be more than just a cataclysm. There has to be a plot. And there have to be people or something (artificial intelligences, animals, aliens, zombies, cannibals, etc.), with which the readers can identify and through whom they can vicariously live the horrors of whatever apocalypse that you, as the writer, choose.

Now, what agency or type of Armageddon should you select? Well, the list is virtually endless. Disease (as in "Earth Abides") is a great one for horror stories, because this topic allows for those zombies! Also, ice ages, sun going nova, earth exploding, and worlds colliding, have all been done many times and often very well. Right now, comets impacting Earth are big, but in my opinion, overdone. Same with nuclear holocausts (there have been lots of those, and they are good for after-the-fact fantasy settings), and alien invasions (every type of creature imaginable has attacked the earth—from blobs to "Bobs" and these are also good for horror settings), and now global warming.

There have been literally thousands of stories on all these subjects.

Does this mean that you shouldn't use these particular end-of-the-world scenarios? No, it does not. But it does mean that if you want to stand out, rather than just ending as another run-of-the-mill writer (probably unpublished), you will need a fresh approach. You need to be unique. So if your story is about a nuclear holocaust, for instance, then try something other than the old and dreadfully stale "what lucky persons get to be in the bomb shelter and survive, while everyone else gets to die" routine.

Why not write it, instead, from the viewpoint of a mentally handicapped woman living in an institution when these events occur, or a born-again preacher seeing it through religious eyes? How would apocalypse unfold for a robot servant? What would people of some isolated region, like the mountains of New Guinea, do if suddenly outsiders stopped coming, and they had to cope with radiation? What might be the end of our world just might simply be a return to their old world! You see? Give it a new angle. Explore the human, alien, or artificial intelligence psyche. In the final analysis, all of them are really us, you know. For science fiction and horror, this sort of approach is fantastic. But don't forget fantasy either. Settings, such as many of those created by Andre Norton, are great for this, and you can throw in horror there, along with science fiction, as well. She was a master at cross-genre blending in this respect.

And Armageddon doesn't have to be just on an earthly scale. It can be spread across star systems, galaxies, and even the universe. Don't use too narrow a definition on what an apocalypse, or end-of-the-world situation might be. The end-of-civilization-as-we-know-it may be more subtle; more of an emotional/horror nature, but it can still be just as devastating for the people involved. Or, try using a twist or surprise ending. For instance, how about a story of invasion by an alien empire which is brutal, unforgiving, destructive, and which turns out to be us, humans?

Do pay close attention to the details of the type of holocaust that you use. Make darn sure they are technically correct. Research it—a lot! For instance, during ice ages, it wasn't all ice and woolly mammoths. There were also large expanses of desert. Beware of obvious pitfalls, as in the movie, **Armageddon**. It was fun and fast-paced, but all those house-sized boulders bouncing harmlessly off Bruce Willis' space shuttle? Come on! Remember the flooding of New York caused by global warming in the movie, "A.I.?" When the ice age came, that water froze around the buildings instead of retreating as it should have done! Warm periods, sea levels rise — frigid periods, they fall. Oops! And those zombies in **28 Days**, and such? Would someone explain to me how eating living flesh keeps dead things alive, and turns live people into zombies, please? The horror in that movie was good, but the premise (as with so many zombie movies in my opinion), was weak.

But Armageddon, whatever its nature, is truly seen through the eyes of the beholders. So it is up to us to make it exciting, interesting, frightening and disturbing—in other words, a good read. And like those terrible comets, it should also have a **Deep Impact**! And that holds true whether it is pure science fiction, sci-fi horror, horror, or even fantasy.

CHAPTER 19

The Dangers of Time Travel

Time travel is an exceedingly dangerous form of travel. This is especially so for authors of science fiction, fantasy, or horror. By comparison, a simple warp drive, or hyper drive, is a Sunday walk in the park, a far safer method of getting from here to there across the multiverse. Yes, nasty accidents do occur in stories with faster-than-light (FTL) ships, but need I point out that those horrible happenings transpire only in the stories themselves, and affect only the characters there? Whereas, time travel can maim or even kill an author, at least in the career-sense.

How is this possible? Well, with time travel there is much that lies in wait for the unsuspecting, unwary writer. Where once we authors pretty much didn't have to even worry about this subject (last couple of decades or so, at least), because editors weren't crazy about publishing time travel stories (infamous quote from one editor: "they've been done"), things have now changed. The literary landscape has suffered from several time quakes in recent years. It has undergone a profound transformation in a number of ways as a result.

What caused this? There are several reasons. First, over the last few years, the so-called "impossibility" of time travel, at least as far as quantum physics theories go, seems to be breaking down—considerably. This makes the subject in fiction less taboo to those various hard-line editors that want only "hard SF."

Secondly, there are now some interesting new story concepts and ideas, because of these new types of theories, with regard to time travel, and other related anomalies. These ideas intrigue editors. Darn it! (Just more for us authors to have to think and worry about, in my opinion.) So editors now seem more susceptible of late to accepting such time travel stories based on such notions. Worse luck for us, because that means we have to write the nasty little things and we have to be oh-so-careful while doing it. With time travel, the devil is in the details—always!

And thirdly, seldom if anything much is ever done for authors in the way of training them to write time travel tales. We, as writers of science fiction, horror, or fantasy, are taught little about the problems and intricacies of it, tech-wise and plot-wise, beyond constantly having the all-too-obvious "Grandfather Paradox," restated to us. And, I'm sure we authors are all too well aware of that particular little conundrum. If we're not, our editors are quick to point that fact out to us when they read our tales. And, if you don't know what the Grandfather Paradox is, then shame on you! Just Google it on the internet and plenty will come up about it—I assure you.

Now, why am I "harping" on the subject of time travel? Why is a simple trip to the past or future so fraught with literary loss for an author's career? Well, the answer is simple; time travel is tricky! It's very devious.

And yet, all forms of time travel seem to be in vogue again, and especially alternate reality versions of time stories. Editors have a newly reawakened interest in them. I suspect this simple fact may be due to the public having had a reawakened interest in them first. If the public rediscovers something, editors soon follow.

Case in point: *The Yiddish Policemen's Union*, by Michael Chabon. This alternate universe (reality) book debuted in 2007 and made it to the New York Times' Bestsellers List almost immediately, among other such lists, and is even now supposedly in preproduction as a movie adaptation. The novel has won every kind of science fiction award one can imagine, including the *Sidewise Award for Alternate History, Nebula, Hugo*, etc.

In other words, this book is selling, baby! And selling big! Editors' little ears all over the world have pricked up upon hearing this, and so, time travel, alternate histories in particular, are suddenly very trendy.

And that's bad news for us writers, because now we have to write them. And unlike FTL stories, which we can pretty much make up any old way we want to, as long as we have a good plot, characters, exotic settings, and pace; time travel related stories aren't nearly so neat or easy to construct.

The main problem seems to occur with stories about trips to the past, or alternate history stories of the same ilk. These require research—lots of it. And believe me, if you don't do it, the type of readers who are fascinated with these topics will point it out to you quickly enough—so will the editors! So, to do alternate history stories, or time travel tales set in the past, the first thing an author must be aware of is:

1. Do your research. Know the time period you are talking about in as much detail as possible. This can be problematic. It's the little things that can trip you up. For instance, did carriages in the 17th century have spring supports to make the traveling in them easier? Did they have these in the 15th century? What did people in England eat for breakfast in 18th Century England? Did it differ markedly from what they ate in the 19th? When did chimneys become commonplace? (They weren't always, you know.) How many tines did forks have in the 14th Century? Did they even use forks then? And if so, where? See what I mean—you had better know your subject matter.

And don't think that being set in an alternate history universe means you can fudge on these factors. As in Michael Chabon's popular piece, the settings had better be clear, fixed, and factual. Michael really had to research his history on the formation of the modern state of Israel, because in his story, it failed to happen. He carefully had to point out why and then he made realistic projections as to what then might occur.

So, he had to not only really know his history on the subject, but he had to understand the politics, primary movers, and social pressures of the times. Then, in a political science sense of extrapolation, he had to tell us where all this might lead in a "today's" alternate world. Not easy!

And don't forget that with time travel stories, despite some new interesting theories in quantum mechanics that seem to allow for them as a reality, hard science fiction editors still want to "be convinced," as do many of their readers. Just using any old wormhole as a route to the past, future, or even across space, isn't going to cut it these days.

As a story mechanism, it might have worked a decade or so back (Carl Sagan's, *Contact*, for instance), when much wasn't really known by the general public about wormhole theory. But now, things have changed. Wormholes have problems. If they exist at all, they seem to be way too small to send something through, apparently, and there may be a self-fulfilling rule that makes them collapse just before one can send anything. Besides, editors do feel they've been overdone. So, use wormholes at your own risk.

And, did you know that there is talk of building an actual time machine of sorts? University of Connecticut Professor, Ronald Mallet, wants to try and send a subatomic particle through time. The catch is the device can't send something further back in time than his device existed. Also, it may be only information that can be sent—no people. So if you use his device to send someone back to dinosaur land, editors are going to howl—at you, again!

Then there is the Cazimir Effect along with exotic matter as related to time travel. It might work. After all, they used the idea of exotic matter in the television series, **Lost**, didn't they? And it made for some interesting horror aspects, as well. But, well, that show overlooked a few of the finer (*and major*) points on this issue, and to their detriment. I don't know about you, but that show was rather contrived for me as a result, what with moving the island around and all. An island isn't a boat, for gosh sakes! It isn't necessarily going to be stable wherever you happen to just plop down the stupid thing.

But back to the time travel aspects of exotic matter; to travel through time, or space-time, would require a construct of enormous proportions. As Professor Michio Kaku points out, it would involve having a black hole at your disposal, as well as exotic matter to stabilize it, and the whole thing would be at least on the order of Jupiter in size/mass. Now that "ain't gonna" fit on "no island," as "they" say, or even on Earth. So, another thing an author must be very aware of is:

2. Do your research (again!). Time travel, device-wise, had better have some convincing, currently-thought-of-as-feasible method of time travel with which to please the potential editor and now more sophisticated public. You had better be darn sure of any time travel device's limitations, such as size, power source, sending only information, or only sending something back as far as the device was still in existence, and not farther.

And yes, I know this is the exact same rule as my first one ("Do your research"), but that's my point. Research into possible time travel devices is all important, just as it is in knowing the period your characters are being sent to. Whether it is the era you are writing about, or the physical means of traveling through time, past or future—you, as an author, had better know your stuff, had better get it right. And quantum physics theories, by the way, might also allow for literal alternate realities. Getting complicated now, isn't it?

If you want an example of a very bad time travel device, one which the author seemed to go to great lengths to sell to his readers as a realistic one, I suggest you read Michael Creighton's *Timeline*. If you haven't read the novel, then do read it and try to see for yourself why its premise appears so flawed. The problems lie not only with how the time-traveling device functioned (including visually), but with the alternate past/future concepts as elucidated upon in the work. Fuzzy thinking on quantum mechanics there, folks!

And finally, one of the third major problems of time travel stories is that they are still a difficult sell in many respects. Hard science fiction editors might now cast a less-jaundiced eye upon them, but many still have to be "sold" on the idea. It has to seem "believable" to them. Also, alternate history stories abound. There are magazines just devoted to them. It's a crowded field. So, when it comes to selling your time-travel or alternate history story, there is a third point you must remember. Yes, it should seem very familiar by now. When it comes to sending time-travel tales, or alternate history stories to editors, you must:

3. Do your research. Send it to the wrong editor or magazine, and they won't even glance at it. Editors are real picky on this subject. It's a primordial time jungle out there, my fellow authors, and we're all trapped in it like bugs in amber!

In any case, in order to write time-travel tales, or alternate history stories, you, as a writer, must know your stuff! Is there an upswing in a demand for such tales? Oh, yes. And again, since newer quantum theories of time travel now exist that seem "scientifically plausible," editors are allowing for more of such stories. And thanks largely due to Michael Chabon, Harry Turtledove, and others, alternate histories are also getting quite popular.

And don't think that this is just about science fiction. Time travel is extensively used to get people to past settings that are more fantasy than reality. And as for horror, time travel can make for great tales! My *GreenWaters* is a horror story based entirely on the idea of time travel. Although with this story, the means of time travel are visions in nightmares (not breaking any "physical universe" rules this way, you see).

But as always, time travel is still a tough sell. And yes, there can be stories that skip around the above issues—if they are really great stories! Otherwise, like most of us writing hacks, you will just have to pay your dues, research, write, and then hope! Again, details are important in time travel tales. You must tie them up nicely and neatly. A big "no-no" is to leave some important issue just hanging there at the end, unexplained.

A lot to remember, I know, but if you can just remember my three main points here, you can succeed in writing such stories. Again, those points are: **research, research,** and more **research**! When it comes to time travel and alternate history, a writer can't get by without it.

CHAPTER 20

The Awesome Power Of Steampunk

Steampunk is gaining steam and lots of it. More and more, we science fiction, horror, and fantasy authors are being "pressured" to consider writing in this genre, to jump on that particular train ("locomotive?"). Why? Well, Steampunk is spreading and in some rather incredible ways. And there is no point in getting "steamed" about all this, because Steampunk seems to be here to stay for the foreseeable future. Okay, so I've probably pushed the puns to death here, but let's be fair, they are easy to do with this subject, so cut me some slack!

Anyway, when Steampunk first started in the 1980's nobody could have predicted its rapid and very powerful growth. After all, it was just another subgenre among many other old and new genres of sci-fi and fantasy at the time, along with Cyberpunk, Sci-spy, Mundane, Biopunk, New Wave, Science Fiction Westerns, Space Westerns (no; Science Fiction Westerns and Space Westerns aren't the same thing), Gothic Science Fiction, Cosmic Science Fiction, Alternate History, Erotic Science Fiction, Apocalyptic, Post-Apocalyptic, Christian, Gay/Lesbian, Time Travel, Space Opera, Pulp, Military, Horror, New Fantasy—well the list does go on, doesn't it? And it doesn't stop there. Steampunk has infiltrated movies (**Golden Compass, League Of Extraordinary Gentlemen, Bioshock**), anime (**Steamboy**), complete novels, and so much else!

So who knew that Steampunk would be one of the leading contenders? So powerful has it grown that it's now influencing not just fiction, but even art and culture in the form of designs of such things as clothing, homes, and computers! More importantly for us writers, many magazines and publishing outlets want it, some exclusively. And this is true whether it's horror about Jack-the-Ripper, alternate science fiction universes, or pure fantasy tales set in other realities. So wax those keyboards, my fellow authors, and make those fingers fly, because you'd better consider writing something in Steampunk, and this is regardless of whether you write science fiction, horror, or fantasy.

But what is Steampunk? Well, the main definition seems to be anything written in a 19th Century setting or atmosphere with emphasis on the Victorian Period, or style. It is when most things were powered by steam. Think Jules Verne with his Captain Nemo and the submarine *Nautilus*. Ponder H.G. Wells with his airships and such—not to mention that lovingly-upholstered, baroque-and-brass time machine of his. I wanted a model of that!

So instead of our types of computers, you'd probably use analog versions, rather like old fashioned mechanical adding machines, only much more complex, maybe filling an entire building or city block. Instead of jets zooming around, you would use propeller-driven dirigibles. Interoffice communications would be via pneumatic tubes, rather than electric intercom systems. Picture lots of brass fittings, tubing, piping, and steam hissing out of various valves. Envision the odd woman in a hoop skirt and bonnet, dresses with bustles and bows, or a few men in top hats and cravats, and you have the setting. Now toss in a big dollop of science fiction, horror, or fantasy (how about evil fairies existing?) to go with that, and you have—Steampunk!

Perhaps one of the main reasons for the rapid growth of Steampunk is its flexibility. Whether set in an alternate universe, our actual one of the 1800's, on some other planet, some other type of universe, past or present, or just set in a world of pure fantasy, even including magic as a prominent feature, Steampunk seems to not only hold it's own, but apparently is expanding rapidly, as well.

Do not confuse Steampunk with cyberpunk. They may have had the same source, but they are now parallel and pretty much separate movements/subgenres. Yes, there is crossover (slipstream may account for this) involved, but where cyberpunk has a real penchant for failed utopian visions ("dystopia"), Steampunk is usually not nearly so dark in that particular way. It tends to incorporate that joyous feeling of the 19th Century that anything was possible, anything could be invented. However, that doesn't mean Steampunk can't be dark, because it can.

Picture an air war, for instance. It might be composed of fleets of dreadnaught dirigibles, with troops trying to commandeer other "vessels" by gliding across to them using batwing-style personal gliders, as in my novella, *Engine Of The Gods*. Maybe, in such a setting, the definition of a super bomb would be a new type of powerful dynamite, capable of blasting a city center, rather like the American military's MOAB (Mother Of All Bombs, which isn't atomic in nature). See what I mean? It's all fascinating stuff. And it's so fascinating; it's seizing an ever larger portion of the sci-fi or fantasy writing market, so as an author you should think seriously about trying your hand at writing it.

I've always lamented the whole *Harry Potter* phenomenon, which made the subject of magic in general so popular, as well as the vampire trend going on today. This wasn't because I didn't like them, but because I didn't get in on the ground floor, missed these two in their early development. In other words, when it came to surfing trends in science fiction and fantasy writing, I missed the wave! And frankly, the *Harry Potter* magic types of novels, those wonderful fantasies, although still popular, do seem to have definitely peaked. And, with everyone and their sister writing vampire and werewolf romances, erotica, adventures, and urban fantasies of the same ilk, it seems we will soon be peaking there, as well, if not already.

But Steampunk is still growing. It offers fantastic opportunities for horror and fantasy writers, as well as for science fiction authors. And believe it or not, many writers haven't really heard of it, or if they have, either they don't know what it really is, or dismiss it as just another niche genre. Well, I don't think so. Again, it's growing rapidly and well may make a major showing for some time to come in our writing sphere.

For example, hosts of magazines are doing "Steampunk weeks," "Steampunk issues," and such promotions. One site, **Galaxy Express** at:

http://www.thegalaxyexpress.net/2008/09/steampunk-is-new-black.html

(This may no longer be an active link at time of printing of this book) refers to "Steampunk as the new black!" As the article says, lots of folk are blogging about it, "spreading the buzz," and it is "showing up in more books and films." There is even a **Steampunk Magazine**. So it is my opinion, my educated guess that the Steampunk train is leaving town, and if you aren't on it, you'll be missing the "steamboat." Yes, there I go in, but really it is just so easy to make these sorts of puns…

As **Galaxy Express** says:

> *Steampunk*— *"It's stylish, involving lots of shiny brass and oversized rivets." And readers, often like children, are attracted to "shiny" things.*

And you as a science fiction/fantasy/horror author had better be able to supply it when they want it. That's the catch here; you have to be riding that groundswell, not splashing about, at literary sea, somewhere behind the curve. Trust me; there's money to be made in steam, folks, so do think about writing Steampunk. Whether your interests lie in horror, fantasy, sci-spy, time travel, or even Space Westerns, Steampunk settings are still easily used, and can be a good integral part of your story. Steampunk is big on atmosphere. It may get a little misty at times as a result, but hey, nothing's perfect! And yet for horror, that is perfect! Well, it's just as much for fantasy, as well, I strongly suspect.

CHAPTER 21

Science Fiction, Fantasy, And Horror as Morality Plays

Have you ever watched an old western movie? It's a stupid question, I suppose. I mean, after all, I'm sure the vast majority of us have tuned into them at some point in our lives, if only out of sheer boredom or idle curiosity. Come on, admit it—you know you have; either late at night when nothing else was on television or on that day you took off from work pretending you were sick and didn't dare go outside for fear of someone catching you faking it. (Yeah, you're not alone. We've all done it.)

Those westerns were all remarkably similar in many aspects, weren't they? The good "guys" were dressed in white and the bad "guys" were always dressed in black, if only to make it easier for us to tell them apart. Apparently, in those days, their actions did not speak louder than their costumes. Either that or the moviemakers felt they had particularly stupid audiences, ones that needed strong visual cues to help tell the heroes from the villains. Oh, well!

Of course, night shots were terrible. You'd see the hero dressed in glaring white firing away at a bunch of dark shadows flitting about the place. One had to strain to make out if they were even human, let alone which individual bad guy it was. What a revealing target the hero made in those shootouts! He might as well have painted a bull's eye on his chest, what with all that white he wore. Of course, those champions would always win out eventually, and despite their oh-so-noticeable apparel. They'd go on to trounce the evildoers, and then usually get the fair maiden into the bargain, sort of like a prize handed over for the best gunner at a turkey shoot. And there you have it, the age-old morality play.

It sounds so out-of-date, not to mention so terribly incorrect, politically, with regard to objectifying women as prizes, doesn't it? But dress that bad boy up as Darth Vader (wearing black), and the hero as Luke Skywalker (wearing white, no less), put them in a science fiction setting, and old morality plays get a whole new lease on life.

And this holds just as true for fantasy. You will have the "Dark Wizard" and the "White Wizard," the "Good Queen," and the "Bad Queen." Whether knights, sorcerers, various forms of royalty, or whatever, fantasy is really pulling the same thing in that it is all about morality plays, good versus evil, etc. And horror more often than not fits this same bill. That "monster" is evil. And the heroes (male and female), must struggle against all odds to survive despite it. So whether it is horrible aliens, horrible sea creatures, or horrible serial killers, again, we're talking about the same basics of good against evil, or innocence against corruption. This isn't just a one-shot deal. It works over and over in books and movie, after movie, after movie! The **Star Wars** saga, for example, has spanned decades. **Harry Potter** movies have spanned at least a decade, and then there are movies like **Lord Of The Rings**, and so it goes and continues to go. And those films have made oodles of money. Talk about a cash cow (boy?).

So, what's that old cliché about "all things change, but remain the same?" When it comes to what sells, apparently this would seem to be true. Moreover, it works for books just as well as movies.

Now, why is that do you suppose? Are we no different in our belief systems from our parents, grandparents, or even great grandparents? (Please feel free to go back as far as you like here.) Are we just cardboard copies of all those who came before us, and so doomed to just "strutting our stuff" on the same tired stage, in the same old way? Have we nothing new to add to aging ideas. Do all we have are stale concepts about morality, or what is "right?" Science fiction, fantasy, horror—is much of it condemned to be a constant rehash of what came before with just different trappings?

The answers to all these questions are a definite yes and no. (What—you wanted definitive, black-and-white answers on questions concerning something as esoteric as morality? Good luck with that one!) However, maybe we should first define what we mean by a morality play.

Historically, these medieval plays had the characters in them actually representing such things as good, bad, death, etc. Inspired by the Catholic Church of the period, they were to teach valuable moral lessons. E.g., only those who are good can triumph or receive rewards (see; "getting the girl"), or that gluttony and excess were evil incarnate.

Sound familiar? It should. And it isn't just old westerns that reflect this type of story morality. Check out the Baron Harkonnen in **Dune**. Sexual excess and gluttony equals evil, diseased, fat man who must die horribly. Notice how when someone strays from the chosen path of righteousness (the Force) he or she becomes evil and lost, as with Darth Vader in **Star Wars**? How does he redeem himself? He does it by making the ultimate sacrifice—dying to save the good "guy." (Get it?) Granted, some of this was done as satire, with a sense of humor about it, but the audience still reacts as if it were deadly serious.

So much of what we have today, albeit with different settings and accoutrements, does mirror that which our ancestors enjoyed many centuries ago. Why is that? Well, probably because our basic belief systems, our moral ideas about right and wrong, haven't changed a whole lot since then. We still have the "seven deadly sins," and we still see certain things as evil and other things as good, much the same as our forebears did. So put the "guy" in white to symbolize good, and the other "guy" in black to symbolize evil, add light sabers and spaceships, sword and sorcery, or manic murderers, and get on with that morality play!

Still, things are changing. No society remains static. Even the religions that existed in medieval times are slowly evolving, undergoing transitions. So, too, are ideas of morality. Now, I suppose that may sound farfetched to some readers of this column. After all, most of us think of the concepts of good and evil as being ultimate terms of rhetoric. That is, they are immutable, unchangeable, something not alterable in any way.

Well, our concepts of good and evil are slowly shifting. Let's take the Baron Harkonnen, for instance. A nationwide poll, taken just last week, now finds that many Americans no longer see being fat as a bad thing. So just because the Baron is a gross overeater, doesn't make him evil anymore, despite the fact that gluttony is one of the "seven deadly sins." And his homosexual tendencies, by society's more tolerant standards of today, no longer necessarily make him a bad person, either. Yes, I know many Americans still view that as wrong, but also, many now don't. That's a big change in just 30 years' time. Of course, the Baron had a nasty habit of torturing and killing the innocent, so we still seem him as a bad apple. He was a character we love to hate.

Now please let me make this very clear, so that I don't get a barrage of nasty letters. My point here isn't to make a political or social statement about any of these changes in our viewpoints being good or bad things. I have no particular agenda, and I'm definitely not trying to promote anything over anything else. That's not the issue here. I'm merely saying that these shifts on how we view supposedly ultimate terms, such as good and evil, are in fact slowly altering with time, and these are just a couple of examples of that fact.

It has happened repeatedly throughout history. Romans thought it perfectly normal to slay thousands of people for entertainment purposes. After all, they were the enemy, social outcasts, and misfits of one sort or another. And by Roman moral standards of the day, they deserved to die. Heck, they made darn good entertainment, to boot!

Of course, when Rome converted to Christianity, this slaughter became an immoral practice and was finally abolished. That's a big shift in moral viewpoint! Our modern and supposedly more enlightened culture now heartily condemns what we see as early Rome's terrible excesses. But by Romans' moral standards of the day, we would appear weak, unfit, and unworthy to be a citizen of mighty Rome.

England's empire of the eighteenth and nineteenth centuries had its own unique morality. Rudyard Kipling referred to the "White Man's Burden," as having to "civilize" natives of colonies whether they wanted that "civilizing" or not, force-fed for their own good, as it were. The fact that the British conquered these "colonies" at the point of a gun or bayonet also seemed perfectly reasonable to Victorian England. It was for a greater good. Now, we see that as "imperialism" and "colonialism," and definitely not the thing to do.

So standards of morality do change, like it or not. Whether these are for the better, I'll leave to your own good judgment. But these changes do allow for us to alter what we write, refine our ideas, and concepts of how we, personally, view the world as authors. If everything now were as clear cut and unalterable as the morality plays of the fifteenth century, then we would be very limited, indeed, in our writing possibilities.

We're lucky. We can present different viewpoints and approaches. For instance, Stephen R. Donaldson's, *The Chronicles of Thomas Covenant the Unbeliever*, say it all, and in the very title! He's an unbeliever, an antihero, and an unwilling participant in doing good works who would give anything not to have to do that. What's more, he's a leper! That, symbolically, is the ultimate symbol of a social outcast. Yet, those books went over, and very well. There were sequels!

So use these opportunities wisely. Don't be afraid to stretch the bounds and limits. If society can redefine what is good, what is right, so can we, at least to a reasonable extent. At the very least, we can explore the bases of these modern values, and perhaps shed some light on their origins, the way they are even now shifting.

Most importantly, it allows us as authors to give greater depth to our characters. They can have a dark side as well as a light one. They don't have to be all dressed in black or white anymore. Some can be ambivalent, or make major, even criminal mistakes. They can even be unlikable in many respects, as with Thomas Covenant. Of course, you must remember to create them so that the reader can still identify with them, still care what happens to them. Our concepts of right and wrong haven't changed so much that we would put up with a truly despicable character as the hero, one that has no redeeming features by today's current moral standards.

Oh, and don't forget what still sells! The good "guys" versus bad "guys" thing is very popular, even now. I enjoy reading such books and watching such movies. The only thing is; do the moviemakers of today still see us as so stupid as actually to have to dress their characters up in black and white? Have we then, as an audience, progressed so little since the Middle Ages? Are we still just an unsophisticated rabble, even after all these centuries? I sincerely hope not. Then, I do like drinking a beer from the can, slouching on the couch, and scratching my belly while watching a hack and slash movie, so maybe they're right…DOH!

CHAPTER 22

Promoting Your Writing And The *Book Trailer™*

Okay, before we even get started here, let us be clear on one point; it seems the term, "**Book Trailer™**" is a registered trademark. This is according to a number of sources. Wikipedia, for one, says:

> *"The term Book Trailer is currently a trademarked term owned by Sheila Clover of Circle of Seven Productions."*

Many websites mention this fact, including a number that allow for trailer uploads (some free, some not). However, why someone would want to trademark this is another question entirely…oh, well!

And yes, from now on, I'm using "trailer" since I quickly get tired of inserting "™" because it slows me down. Yeah, I'm lazy—so sue me! And okay, once in a while I'll probably do it just for the heck of it. Satisfied?

Alas, I digress yet again! Anyway, other terms that are now in use are also "book wrap," and "book video," with that last, admittedly, sounding a little confusing, since one could think of a "book video" as being like an "audio book," which it isn't at all. It's just a video blurb for a novel, not the whole novel in video form. That would be known as a *"movie."* Get it? Hmm maybe I'll trademark that! Just kidding.

Seriously though, "trailers" are a relatively new phenomenon. They only started at or near 2002, and didn't become really popular until the advent of such sites as **YouTube**, **Facebook**, **MySpace**, and such. These sites made for easy uploading of videos and at no cost. And they seem to have huge potential audiences. What's more, when a trailer is uploaded on one site, other video sites often automatically link to it, so the darn things are all over the web in no time at all! So, with those new and promising venues for videos established, a new marketplace as it were, **Book Trailers™** took off.

Now, for those not in the know, the *"non-cogniscenti,"* as it were, let's define what a **Book Trailer™** really is. Basically, they can be any length, but the more common, garden-variety, stick to two minutes or thereabouts—often less. They are multimedia blurbs for novels or even short stories, for any kind of work of fiction, or even those of fact, for that matter.

They are meant as a promotional device to help sell a book. The more typical trailers are like a slideshow presentation, with some cool photographs strung together, neat transitions between them, titles, and maybe music to enhance the piece, or set a certain mood. Often, trailers can even be animated versions, flash video sequences, and/or even live-acted ones. Sometimes, authors themselves, or hired professionals, narrate the pieces.

In short, there is a lot of variety to them. There are even **Book Trailer™** awards now. And major publishers use them, as well. An important point here is that a portion of a story simply read aloud by the author is not necessarily a book trailer for award purposes. Keep that in mind if you are trying for one of these awards. But the upshot of all this is that although a very new medium, the trailer phenomenon is a popular and fast growing one!

Now, why is that? Well, as I am always mentioning, it's a heck of a crowded market out there! Everyone is vying to be heard—shouting to be heard actually, over the continuing deluge and din of advertising, just in order to attract the consumer's attention, just to get their stuff sold. So trailers for books have a good advantage.

1. They are audio-visual and people like that. Trailers are quick, easy to view, and often high impact and stimulating.

2. They are usually short, so they work perfectly for today's limited attention span of the consumer. Now, don't get me wrong here. I'm not knocking consumers. Consumers have a limited attention span, because there is so much they have to take in. They simply can't spend a lot of time on any one advertisement.

3. Trailers are more often than not, cheap to produce (very cheap if you do it yourself, but perhaps a little time-consuming). They hit a wide market and are a relatively innovative new way to attract the reading consumer in the form of a multimedia production. And innovation is always important. Novelty is always fun. Plus, the mass marketing side of things works! I've had as many as a hundred hits in one day on a trailer. Does that translate into sales? I'm honestly not sure. I don't think anyone is yet.

Nowadays, the big majority of consumers start their search for many things on the Internet. So the Internet is naturally a good place to showcase and market your work.

Trailers don't require a lot of effort once completed, or any maintenance. Once uploaded, they continue to do their job on their own—promoting your story, without any more help from you. And incidentally, trailers establish more links to an individual author, and spread their name around the Internet more through this process. For instance, type in "Shelsky Where Worlds Collide," and you'll notice my **Book Trailer™** pops up on a number of really unrelated sites because of key words.

So, you can see there are a number of reasons why trailers are becoming so popular. Of course, there is one more for me—I can't help but check out my competition's trailers to see how they compare with my own. Some are pretty darn impressive! But for me, the most important reason to do trailers is that they quickly get my work out to a wide consumer audience. Trailers showcase my work and me. It's a great form of cheap but apparently powerful PR (Public Relations). It's as simple as that.

Now, what's the best way to do a **Book Trailer™**? Well, there are a number. You can hire someone else to create one just for you—pay them in other words, or you can do it yourself, or even collaborate with several others. I recommend that if you are short on cash and are principally doing your own public relations work, as most of us authors are, to try doing them yourself. They are easy. Here's how to do a basic one:

1. Start with a program like Windows Movie Maker (comes with most basic Windows programs, XP, etc. Powerpoint is another good one, and there are many others. Most of us have some version of one of these already, and if not, and you don't have the money to buy such, check out freeware or shareware sites for public domain programs. These are free and legal programs. You must abide by their restrictions.

2. Assemble a series of photos and/or pictures you wish to use. Upload these to the program. And now using that program, add them to the timeline in the appropriate order you wish them to appear. Left to right is the usual way to add them ("click and drag"), just as you want them to appear in order when finished. Just like a slideshow!

3. Include titles. These can be inserted prior, on the actual picture(s), or after the picture(s). Many programs, such as Windows Movie Maker, even have beginning and end credit titling features. Titles can be made to scroll upwards, appear as moving banners, "explode," "zoom" in or out, etc. So, you can sort of animate your trailer in this way. However, keep in mind that titles should be high contrast, clear, and last long enough for the reader to read them. Linger on important titles longer than the less important ones (e.g., where to buy your work!).

4. When you have your photos in order, and all the titling completed, then think about creating specific music and/or narration. Again, there are a number of custom programs that help with this, including top-of-the-line ones you must pay for, or shareware ones you can legally download for free. It might take some searching, but trust me, there are some good free programs out there. And most importantly, it's legal to use them as long as you, again, abide by the noted restrictions. Tailor the length of your music to exactly match the time length of your video. Make sure it is appropriate music for the piece.

5. Some programs allow for more than one audio track. A simple stereo program allows for two. So, you can do background music on one track, and a voice over, or narration on the other track. Then load it into the movie maker program. (Windows Movie Maker has recording capability, as well.)

6. Special effects are common with many of the slideshow or movie making programs. As mentioned above, you can then do some really cool transitions from one slide to the next, but also you can change the appearance of the actual slide. Windows Movie Maker allows for "aging" a picture, "blurring," "zooming," "fading," and all sorts of other things. Powerpoint does as well. So, combine these video effects with the video transition effects, and you have a very animated looking movie when done, even though in reality it's only a series of still pictures. Of course, you can use actual video, too, if you wish!

7. <u>MOST IMPORTANTLY</u>, keep your trailer short! Two minutes or better, even less, is the sweet spot. Again, consumers don't have a lot of time to watch anything these days. And too long a trailer can become tedious, and cause the consumer to "tune out." Also, uploading time limitations and restrictions on file size will come into play if your video is too large. Many sites, including **YouTube**, limit file size, although these are getting better of late. They allow a lot of leeway in this, but still there are limits. But it is the general public's attention span, which should be your biggest concern. Remember to add "tags." Keywords help people search better for your trailers. Put in as many keywords as allowed.

When you are done, you should have a nice, two-minute, or less, movie. Now, most sites allow for these movies to be in standard mpeg format, but some prefer flash, or others formats. If in doubt, check out their requirements by going to such sites, and seeing what they require. There are freeware programs you can download to convert your format to those others.

Once uploaded, you've done your job. But make sure you upload in fairly high quality. Many sites "process" a movie and it then becomes less in resolution. So, if you start with low resolution to begin with, by the times its processed you may end up with a blurry mess of a movie. The more sites you upload the same movie to, the better, In just a few days, extra links will appear when you run a search program on it (**Google**, **Yahoo**, etc.), and most of these sites do "count" the number of hits you get. Trust me, you'll get quite a number. I find that **YouTube** works best, along with **Facebook**. **Yahoo Video**, for me personally, wasn't so great.

Finally, do remember that any pictures, photos, or music you use must either be copyright or royalty free, if not your own work. There are sites where one can download royalty-free music, and stock photo sites as well. But remember, as an artist (and writers are artists!), you must not step on, or infringe upon other artists' rights, copyrights, or royalty rights in any way. So be aware of this point, and don't do it! After all, you wouldn't want someone to do it to you!

And, if you want my own examples of two **Book Trailers™** (a little self-promotion here!) that I've done, here they are:

Avenger of The People Trailer:

http://www.YouTube.com/watch?v=QosUchKP7LA

Where Worlds Collide Trailer:

http://robshelsky.blogspot.com/p/video-trailers.html

Actually, the above isn't really about self-promotion in this case, but rather it's to give you an idea of what a basic, easy-to-do trailer looks like. And they show some of my first mistakes—titles that come and go too quickly, and wrong contrasting colors for them, etc. You'll notice the *Where Worlds Collide* one is considerably more professional looking than the *Avenger Of The People* one. But, they will give you a good idea of the basic **Book Trailer™** format. (See? It never hurts to promote yourself, even if badly—"there's no such thing as bad publicity!" Right? Hmm….)

And one last important point; many of these sites automatically give you the "embedding code" to then embed the video on your home web page or elsewhere, as I've done above with *Where Worlds Collide*. It's quick, simple, and a great way to make your home website look better. And it's more links, ergo, more promotion for you!

So, when it comes to doing PR, whether you do it yourself, or have others do it for you, don't forget the **Book Trailer™.** Again, it's a very cheap, high impact way to promote yourself and your work.

Try it! In addition, don't forget to put those trailer links in all your emails to everyone, right after your signature line. You'd be surprised how many people are just curious enough to click on them. Moreover, most of all good luck with your PR endeavors. It's an important part of being an author now, and an unavoidable one. So, get used to it. Make a movie!

CHAPTER 23

Science Fiction And Fantasy As Think Tanks

Science Fiction; full of weird ideas, isn't it? The genre is chocker block full of strange notions, bizarre concepts, and outrageous opinions about everything from evolution, nature of the universe, politics, religion, societal structures, and so much more. Actually, to a large extent, so is fantasy. This is what makes science fiction and fantasy such fascinating genres. They are often intriguing, spellbinding ones just for this reason. To be able to investigate all these things in the form of stories is a powerful attraction for readers and moviegoers. Sci-fi and fantasy authors create scenarios, plots, and characters in all these realms and then explore them, each author in his/her own particular way. And we readers go right along with them for the ride. It's fun. It's entertaining. It's exciting. It's disturbing—sometimes very disturbing. But usually, it's something of a learning experience, as well.

However, we must not lose sight of the main thing. Above all else, and it is something most of us tend to overlook since it's so obvious, science fiction and fantasy are profound generators of ideas. They both form massive think tanks. Science fiction constantly and persistently takes old ideas and reshapes those thousands of ways, and envisions entirely new scenarios, ones based often on completely new thought concepts. By this, I mean new ideas, of course. And, incredibly, these new ideas, and radically re-envisioned old ones, often shape our physical reality around us to an extent we usually don't realize. This is immediate to us, not some abstract notion. This is real. It affects us every day in our daily life. And it's all due to fantasy and science fiction.

Case in point; the television show, **Star Trek**; I'm sure a lot of us have seen the two-hour special **How William Shatner**

Changed The World. I watched **Star Trek** as a kid. Even then, articles in various magazines, such as *TV Guide,* and others discussed the impact this television show had on the real world. For instance, at the time, the U.S. Navy was intrigued by the idea of designing bridges of their ships, using the design of the Enterprise's bridge as a template. They sent representatives to visit the set, because it seemed such a good way to arrange a bridge, with everyone stationed in a semicircle around the captain, and all at their own stations. Since then, they've done just that.

Some hospitals liked the announcement sound that ship communicators made, that annoying "chirp." They even used it, saying it cut through background noise better than what they had at the time. They also liked the idea of diagnostic beds, such as Doctor McCoy used in his "sick bay."

And everybody wanted those sliding doors! At the time (and many don't remember this because they weren't born then) automatic doors swung inward or outward, they didn't slide from side-to-side. Investigators, upon contacting the show, were disappointed to find out that hidden staff, off-screen, pulled the doors back and forth by hand. The "shooshing" sound was dubbed in.

But guess what? We have those doors now, and it doesn't take invisible people to operate them. We also have the cell phone, another direct outgrowth of efforts by "nerds" who first saw these ideas on Star Trek and then grew up wanting to replicate them for real. Automatic diagnostic devices, such as left-right brain scanners are now a fact, along with CAT scanners, MRI scanners, and so many other new medical devices. And if you watch that two-hour show on how William Shatner (really **Star Trek**) changed the world, you will see a host of other such "wonders," that now form part of our everyday physical reality. Remember, they didn't physically exist when they were first portrayed on **Star Trek**. They were just science fiction "ideas."

And the same goes for fantasy. Architectural designs have become bolder, enlivened by imaginative designs first demonstrated in fantasy stories for houses and various buildings.

The same goes for gardens. Fantasy often plays a big part in shaping many gardens. And so it goes and continues to go.

So do science fiction and fantasy ideas shape our physical reality? You betcha! For instance, one can't get through the day, it seems, without in some respect being impacted by those **Star Trek** ideas. Whether it's a trip to the doctor (scanning devices), Wal-Mart (those sliding doors), or just using your cell phone (starship communicators), your physical reality is directly impacted on a daily basis by what came first on that show. And let's not forget such famous authors as Arthur C. Clarke, whose idea of using satellite communications to create our current "global village." Now it's a fact. Again, so it goes, and continues to go. Sci-fi authors generate idea after idea that later we want to become part of our everyday reality, and so we "make it so," as Jean-Luc Picard liked to say.

But what about the metaphysical; does science fiction and fantasy impact our belief systems, alter our views of eternity, life after death, meaning of life, the ultimate nature of reality, and such, to the same degree? Again, you betcha! Metaphysics literally means "behind the wall of nature," (source, Wikipedia.com). And isn't that what all religions and belief systems do, peer behind the wall of nature, try to give us answers about "everything?"

For countless generations, religions have been our only answer to such fundamental questions, the ones mentioned above in this paragraph. Then science came along and is now trying to do the same. And science fiction and fantasy are no different in this respect. They often postulate what might be "behind the wall of nature," in some way, as well. Sci-fi and fantasy forms their own think tanks, not just for ideas on changing our daily physical reality, but our metaphysical ones, as well.

Besides one glaringly obvious example of this, as with the now-deceased, sci-fi author, L. Ron Hubbard, and his founding of Scientology, a belief system many famous people and others adhere to, there are constant infusions of science fiction ideas into the world of metaphysics.

Just think about how the average science fiction reader gets a steady influx of these new ideas, different perspectives on religion, alternate ideas on the nature of reality, from the SF they read. Readers absorb these ideas. Often, they will incorporate parts of them into their own belief systems. Same goes for fantasy. Many modern belief systems are inherently based on the idea of nature as god or goddess, and such. Even our newfound respect for the environment has partly come about from this sort of thing.

So do new religions and "isms" evolve, ones at least partly based on science fiction and fantasy then? Of course, Scientology is but one current example. Whether one chooses to believe in it or not, many do, as is their right. The same with "New Age" beliefs; these cover a very wide range of ideas, indeed. The sources of some of these ideas directly include science fiction and/or concepts from fantasy as their points of origin.

Need more proof? Even the Catholic Church recently stated that there could very well be other intelligent life in the universe, and this was once strictly against their belief systems, not to be considered, nor to be discussed. So religions, people's beliefs in the metaphysical, change and alter all the time. Science fiction and fantasy influence this by altering the majority of people's opinions about such things as the possibility of the existence of UFOs (majority of Americans now "believe" in them) and so is integral to this ongoing process.

And don't kid yourself; science fiction really has a lot to do with this. If it weren't for the original novel, *War of the Worlds*, by H.G. Wells, the idea of alien intelligent life entering the mainstream world wouldn't have become so prevalent nearly so quickly. It would probably have remained for quite a while longer, perhaps several decades, as just an obscure thought experiment, only exercised by the few, the "intellectual elite" and not the many.

So, like it or not, science fiction directly affects our belief systems as to what we consider possible, probable, and real. It promotes new ideas about it all, suggests new possibilities to be explored, and alternative versions, even in the strictly religious sense. Sometimes, it creates new believers in new faiths, or reaffirms their existing faiths. Other times, it just alters them, or even takes away their old belief systems entirely.

The power of science fiction and fantasy as think tanks for the physical and the metaphysical cannot be overlooked. As profound generators of new ideas, and alternate ways of looking at older ones, these genres can be a powerful tool for change. It creates new viewpoints, new ways of looking at old problems. And, they are not just possible prognosticator of the future. They are helping to shape that very future, that new reality we are moving into, even as we speak, even as we do it, and not just the physical, but the metaphysical as well. Anyway, it's just a thought, an idea, if you will...so when it comes to science fiction or fantasy as a think tank, "tanks" for listening. (Okay, I couldn't resist that.) But remember, you as a writer of these genres are pushing frontiers, pushing the envelope. So consider wisely what you want to say, how you say it, and in what "light" you say it, because it does have a strong effect!

CHAPTER 24

What Are Our Moral Obligations As Writers?

Morality—we've discussed this somewhat before with regard to morality plays—good versus evil, bad guys/girls versus good guys/girls. We've also dwelt some on the subject of censorship versus self-censorship and the problems these pose for us as authors.

However, here we'll go into it in a bit more depth, about the concept of morality itself in our writing. By this, I mean morality as a basic concept when it comes to writing, how we as science fiction, fantasy, and horror authors use it, to what degree should we exercise it?

Let's refine this topic a little, ask a few specific questions here, and see if we can come up with some answers for them.

1. Do we have obligations to write morally sound works, or as authors are we free of such restrictions, can ignore such bourgeoisie social constraints, are above them because we are "artistes?" And,

2. If there were no repercussions, no overt consequences to us as writers, such as lawsuits, editors and publishers shunning our work and us, would we be more likely as a group to write without any moral restraints at all? And should we anyway? Would it hurt or help our readership and/or society if we did this? Does it help to sell our books more, one way or the other?

If, by now, you think we are not going to have conclusive answers to these questions in this chapter, you are probably right! That's pretty much a given. However, the idea here is just to discuss these topics, to bring them to the fore, and give some thought as to what each of us might feel about this particular issue, and how we wish to proceed with writing so as to get published.

Right up front, I think it's obvious that the spectrum of opinion on this issue will be a broad one. It no doubt ranges from those on the far left with an "anything goes," the "sky is the limit" attitude, to those on the far right who believe "we need to be careful about everything we say," to follow strict guidelines, and not to go "against God."

Now, I have to say, I have a little trouble with that last one, because in a multifaceted society, a melting pot such as ours undoubtedly is, it's obvious that we have multiple religions, each with widely different points of view and different beliefs about the nature of just who and what God is, what exactly constitutes "right and wrong." And each such religion believes there viewpoint and belief systems to be absolutely true. That's their right, of course—freedom of religion—and it's a wonderful thing.

But the minute we try to restrict authors of our genres as a group, as to what they can and cannot write according to any one certain set of religious rules, we then run into big trouble because of that wide variety of belief systems. So we must be very careful to realize that this type of religious moral stricture on what we can write, is for each of us, our own individual choice. Others of differing belief systems will not necessarily feel bound by our personal rules, and we will not be bound by their viewpoints.

So when it comes to choosing what we should or shouldn't write, based on religious grounds only—that must, of necessity, be strictly on an individual level, and not applied to the group of science fiction, fantasy, or horror authors as a whole. Why? Because this group has many members with strongly held, but differing beliefs about such matters. And these beliefs should be respected at all times.

Now, just to mention as a side-note; there are many writing outlets, publications, for those who feel this strong, religiously-moral imperative, the need to write only that which is within the bounds of their personal religious beliefs. And if they wish to send it out to publishers in general, as well, I'm firmly convinced that is their right. Sometimes, they may get accepted in such a way.

However, again, it does rather make a problem to try and restrict sci-fi, fantasy, or horror writers by any one set of religious moral strictures. So perhaps then, we need something that all science our writers, *en masse*, can adhere to instead, a central set of guidelines? Could we do this with a set of secular society's moral restraints and guidelines instead of those founded on religious ones?

There's a bit of a problem there, too. Societies are numerous, and so are authors of our genres. I'm personally in touch with many writers from many different parts of the world, and believe me when I say that each society's morals do vary, some in minor degrees, some in major ones! England's moral viewpoint is not the same as Australia, Russia, Norway, or America's standards. For instance, some countries have little or no problem with public nudity.

For others, it's a really big thing! So since we writers are a worldwide community, it seems any one country's set of morals will simply not work for the group as a whole. In this case, one could only go by the country of residence. An American author might go by American standards, as opposed to a German who would go by Germany's standards. The reason for this might even be a legal one—in Germany, for instance, any reference to Nazis is strictly controlled, with even the symbol being banned in most instances. So watch out what you have on your book cover!

So if we went country-by-country, and simply followed such standards for them as our primary place of residence as authors, at least we'd have some system of moral standards by which all authors there could write, some general guidelines, as it were at least on a national level.

Alas, even this isn't the case. The moral standards within countries vary markedly from region to region. Southern California, for example, is in stark contrast to the overall morals of, say, Kentucky. And even if we just take Kentucky, the moral strictures there are greatly in variance between the metropolitan areas, and the extremely rural, hill-country ones. Go just twenty miles out of a city there and it's a completely different world, folks! This is true, at least as far as the moral rules of the societies in such regions are concerned (and often the local dialects, as well).

Okay then, so a set of moral principles based on any one religion must be limited to the strictly individual level, to each person's own set of beliefs. And secular society's moral belief systems vary not only widely from country to country, but from city to city, and even town to town. They are not consistent. So what then can we do as an entire group to have moral guidelines for all, and should we bother?

Ah, now we come again to those questions I earlier mentioned.

To paraphrase, should we have moral obligations to write moral works, or should we write what we want and be damned?

It's tough to answer that one! Again, because of the wide disparity in belief systems, both religious and secular, and depending on region and personal background, the only answer I can come up with is that we must each decide this question for ourselves. Only each of us, individually, can decide what is okay, and what isn't okay to write. But go too far, and our own immediate societies might create a wicked backlash.

For instance, decades ago, in the Sixties, it was **Time Magazine**, I believe, which had a cover that asked: *"Is God Dead?"* The response to this was on a national level. There were two sides of course, but there was a definite negative backlash, no doubt! So, push your particular society or personal group's limits too far, and you may be buying yourself big problems.

Should you do it anyway? Again, that answer can only be on each individual's level. If you personally feel you are making a statement, one which must be made, and so you must chance brooking major repercussions to do it, then that is you choice. If you are just doing it to be doing it—well, that's also your choice, but I do hope you know just how strong the consequences for such an action can be. In some cases, in some countries, and even in certain areas of America, the consequences can even be life threatening.

Now our second question; if there were no such repercussions, such negative consequences, would we as authors go to the extreme and just write about anything and everything, "good," and "bad" (as defined by our particular societies, or religious groups)?

I think we might. Heck, look at television. The more the FCC loosens rules and regulations, the further television shows go. The more they tighten them, the more restricted television shows become.

Whether or not being loose or tight with such restrictions is a good thing, I leave to each reader to determine for him or herself. But I will say this, as much as I loved **"I Love Lucy**," and **"Leave It To Beaver**," as a kid, I now find, upon viewing such shows as an adult in today's world, that they are rather boring, a bit dull, and awfully pontificating at times. Take **"Father Knows Best**," for example. I enjoyed that show. But by today's standards, even that title is irksome and definitely sexist!

Which brings up another point—our societies keep evolving in their moral viewpoints, and we authors often have a lot of influence in that regard. So, push the envelope? Well, the choice is yours. And should we push the envelope? Again, the choice is for each of us personally to decide.

Me, I'm in the middle. There are topics I feel strongly about, and so will push the envelope with regard to them. Others, of less importance to me, I just choose to ignore. And there are some that are like the "third rail!" To touch them is to invite suicide. I only approach these with trepidation, and have to really ponder for a long time if it is even worth "going there!" Again, we must each decide that for ourselves.

I will say this. The concepts of right and wrong, of good versus evil have been with us always as a people, throughout time. And, it is true these concepts have undergone major evolutions in their nature and interpretation, as we've discussed before. Witches, for instance, used to be burned centuries ago. Today, most of us wouldn't think to do that! So, there is nothing so certain as change, as "they" say. And that goes for many of our moral convictions as well, it seems.

In any case, what it all seems to boil down to, morally speaking, is that each of us must search our own consciences, decide for ourselves what our moral principles are, and how and to what degree, if at all, they should affect our writing of science fiction.

Great authors have defied their times and written "morally outrageous" works, only to have their concepts be proven correct by a later generation. Others have written works that were used as foundations for horrible acts by later generations, and I'm talking about science fiction authors here, too!

So, the pen is a powerful sword we wield, folks. And when you write something, it might behoove you to consider the consequences of it, the repercussions for yourself and others, as well. You name may, indeed, echo down through time, but will it be in a "good" way, or bad? And, what will constitute "good" to that later generation? So think before you write. That's the adult thing to do, I think.

Because if we don't put some effort, some thought in to the consequences of our actions, what we write, how it will affect people, not only now but in times to come, we could end up being just like television! And I personally "believe" one "vast desert wasteland" in our society is quite enough. After all, by very definition, authors are literate and literary. And I think we all know, television, except for a few brilliant exceptions, is not! More, so-called reality shows, anyone?

CHAPTER 25

First Contact, A Single Writer's Guide to Meeting Monsters

I'm not a bar hopper, but I have to admit that bars or clubs are where I usually go to find a date. Okay, so I'm clearly labeled a **LOSER** (tattoo it on my forehead, see if I care), but judging by the number of people in any given "hot spot" on a Friday night, I'm not alone. Those joints are overflowing with us. So, one would think the main hurdle of making first contact would be over. They say, "like attracts like," and here we all are, packed in close quarters, sweating, and desperately seeking Susan or Shawn, or whatever….

And you know what? Seldom (okay, okay, so I'm a double loser, I admit it), do I actually find someone this way. Judging by the large number of those going home alone, I'm not unique. Think of it; seven billion people on this planet and counting, and a heck of a lot, if not the majority of them, trying to find a significant other, and failing most of the time. Now there's a depressing thought! (For you "couples" out there, please feel free to insert a smug smirk of superiority here.)

That's where aliens come into it. No, I don't mean as dates (although, some of mine *might* have been…), but with the problem of—you guessed it—first contact! Took a while for me to get around to the topic, didn't it?

Anyway, think about it; we can't make first contact with members of our own species in a confined space, under convivial and alcohol-lubricated conditions, and we're perplexed as to why we can't make contact with other intelligent species in an infinite universe? Come on! Out there, it may not just be the matter of being in the wrong club (see; particular solar system), but the wrong galaxy or super cluster—local or otherwise!

On the vast scale of the universe, we sentient species may be a little sparse, perhaps, not even one per galaxy. Some say there are no other intelligences out there at all. Other say there are plenty, but can't answer the reason for Fermi's "Great Silence." (Translation: no background bar chatter, or in this case, no radio signals from "out there.") And some of these rare races quite probably bloom and die long before, or long after we humans are on the scene, which exacerbates the problem even more (See; Frank Drake's Equation for the likelihood of intelligent life). Therefore, we don't just have to find them, but we have to find them alive.

Still, despite such harrowing obstacles as distance and time, the concept of meeting an alien race enthralls us. Moreover, unbelievably, it may be for much the same reason we seek companionship at a bar. That is, because *we do not like being alone.* We don't even like the *idea* of being alone, and this may be part of our basic genetic makeup. Political Science, for instance, sums this up as one of the underlying precepts of why we behave the way we do: "Humans are social animals." We need to interact. And, that's one reason why stories of first contact are so popular. We like the *idea* of meeting others, even if they have tentacles (See; some of my better dates, or how many women feel about *their* dates).

We do have one thing in our favor; if there are other races out there and they aren't just out exploring space to find planets to populate, then they may be like us in at least one respect; that is, they may be social animals, (or whatever), also. They could be actively looking for first contact just as we are. Therefore, although it's possible *"we are not alone,"* there may be so few intelligent species that *we are all lonely* and thus, seeking others. So literally, where there's life, there's hope (maybe) of making such contact.

When writing stories, keep in mind that this "hands/tentacles reaching across the universe" approach may apply. However, what makes first contact stories fresh are the buildups, the increasing suspense, the speculative marvel, and wonder of it all.

That's not to say that contact tales have to come out well. In sci-fi, many if not most, don't. H.G. Wells' novel, *War of the Worlds* is one classic example. Numerous others are in that vein. Many authors have aliens that are horrors personified. They seem intent only on conquering or consuming us. It turns out they aren't lonely, just belligerent and hungry! William Barton's book, *When Heaven Fell*, falls into this category. It's an intriguing story, one that focuses on how humanity tries to continue behaving as moral beings, even under the tyrannical rule of terrible aliens. Carl Sagan's, *Contact*, is in the opposite vein, where a great interstellar civilization, far above us morally and socially, initiates a tentative first contact with us. As you can see, there are many approaches to writing these stories.

One difficulty is that authors usually have to include global reactions to the discovery of other intelligences. This can involve such negative aspects as riots, religious extremists, panics, and so forth. Would these things happen? Sure, they would, to some greater or lesser degree. But if not handled carefully, this aspect can steal the focus away from the actual contact. Carl Sagan's novel revolves heavily around humankind's reactions. Too much, to my way of thinking, because I was much more eager to meet the aliens than deal with all that. Still, he held up a social mirror in which to view ourselves, and if we don't like the reflection in it… that's just too bad!

If all this first contact stuff is too much for you, well then, you can always seek out some solace at your local club. I'm betting you'll find plenty of alien types there! I happen to know an infamous little dive on the planet Tatooine that's fun, if a little rough. **Star Wars**, anyone?

CHAPTER 26

Conclusion—Evolution and Transcending

Evolution; is it a thing of the past? Has it been done? Are those who think it still works for humans just so many old fossils? Some scientists think so. They point to the idea of the rise of the future "unihuman" where all races of humanity blend into one. They argue that the geographical isolation necessary for different gene pools to develop is no more, that we are now becoming one vast and mixed genetic sea, losing variation because of our "global village" status as a species. Do we need a blatant example of this? Well, with regard to our loss of cultural diversity, Stuart Pimm, of Duke University, says, "…we humans speak something on the order of 6,500 languages. If we look at the number of languages we will likely pass on to our children, that number is 600."

Now, that's one heck of a dramatic and quick reduction in diversity! So, if we are passing on to our children so much less culturally, because of our worldwide blending, the same could very well hold true genetically. Many scientists think this is so. For them, it's a case of, "I have seen the future" and it is a unihuman, with sameness in characteristics dominating throughout our species. This might portend less resistance to sudden viral mutations and other natural challenges. At present, some populations have relative immunity to certain illnesses while others do not. This helps humanity's survival strategy as a whole. If we all genetically become the same, will this still be true? Could some new flu virus in the future cause a worldwide pandemic, decimating the human race, reducing our numbers to a mere handful? Science fiction authors have often written on this very subject in depth and to good effect. *Earth Abides*, by George R. Stewart, is one classic example of such a novel. There are many others, including one by Stephen King. Moreover, such a scenario could become a real danger in our near future, no longer the stuff of science fiction.

But what about the power of science? Will it take over where the global village has left off? Are we destined for a massive evolutionary jump, perhaps one induced artificially? Will we, as a race, or even as individuals, transcend to some higher form of being(s)? Now there again is the stuff of science fiction! Yet, there are signs it may rapidly become fact.

Changing humanity genetically is something we can do right now. We all know that. The list of how we can do that is getting to be a long one. We have cloning capabilities, genetic engineering, *in vitro* fertilization, and we can create mutations through many methods such as by radiation and chemical means. Scientists have even recently devised an embryo with its genetic material capable of coming from just two men or two women, instead of a combination of the two! A race of only one gender — now there's a wild idea, and it, too, has been the subject of books, movies, and even television shows. We genetically treat people with debilitating diseases to stop the progress of such illnesses, or even eradicate them altogether. There have been some very positive results in this endeavor already. And of course, there are all the fears and problems that go with these discoveries. Will we create a super race? Eugenics, that dreaded term first brought to our attention by the monster, Adolph Hitler, may soon come back to haunt us again, and this time for real!

Moreover, let's not forget the cybernetic approach to transforming or transcending humanity. Scientists, in conjunction with doctors, are creating ways right now for the blind to see, the deaf to hear, the paralyzed to walk. They have even wired some test subjects to control machinery directly by thought! These things are no less than true miracles by the standards of only one generation ago (meaning mine). If we extrapolate on this trend, we could create humans who can see most of the spectrum, not just the little slice currently visible to the human eye. The same could happen for hearing, with our range extended way beyond its current limits. And why stop at making people walk again? Could we not build better humans who might lift heavier objects, run faster, jump higher, or swim farther? Shades of the Six Million Dollar Man, right, but why stop there? We could go on to create human beings that might live on other worlds, under other conditions, in other atmospheres, or even in our own seas. Scientists might trigger a human "biospera" where, as a species, we proliferate out into space, colonizing all available worlds by modifying ourselves to fit them. Authors write numerous stories on this subject, as well.

Finally, let's not forget computers and artificial intelligence. The future of the human race might lie in that direction. It's conceivable that we might upload our entire civilization, run it at a faster rate, and create our own in-house realities more to our liking. We could transfer our minds to machines, robots, star ships and sail the vacuous seas of space for near eternity, or even become beings of pure energy, feeding on suns. Again, science fiction authors have dwelt on these subjects. They've done it often and at length.

So where does this leave us as writers? I'd guess it's where it's always left us, cast adrift in a sea of the impossible, or sailing into the realms of the barely plausible. That's our job. We sci-fi authors steer a narrow course, and if we're lucky, land upon the shores of the infinite unknown, perhaps, even making them a little more known!

Yes, it is true that sci-fi authors have already covered these subjects in many ways, shapes, and forms. That's a given. Arthur C. Clarke, and his, *Childhood's End,* is another demonstration of this idea. Nevertheless, there is room for so much more! There are so many aspects of these topics yet to be covered, so many facets of the human condition waiting our exploration and examination. It's our job as science fiction writers to bring these facets to light.

How do we do that? How do we approach such a complex subject, when no scientist even wants to touch on the idea of the future evolution of humanity? Well, we do it in the way we story tellers always have. That is, we use our imaginations to create a scenario and then go with it. It can be any or a combination of all of the above-mentioned ideas, or something else that you, as a writer, have thought up entirely on your own. Ask yourself questions about how some trend may affect humanity and have impact on certain individuals in particular. Think about how the ramifications, the consequences of any of these possibilities (probabilities?), and what effect they might have for people living during their unfolding. Then tell us a story about them.

In addition, remember, just as our future as a species faces countless possible scenarios, innumerable obstacles concerning our survival, and a seemingly endless number of questions regarding pitfalls in relation to that survival, so too are there an equal measure of ideas for us, as science fiction authors to write about and to good effect. And, not only will you be telling a good story, but you might be doing humanity a service. To point out a hole in the road ahead is often to help the driver avoid it. Unless, of course, that driver is one who is particularly obstinate. Then, even that makes for a good story...

CONCLUSION

In conclusion, to be a good writer, you must know the art of writing thoroughly. So as mentioned several times here, constantly practice your craft. Do follow the guidelines in this book carefully. Use the five steps to getting published shown in Chapter 1. Follow the advice given throughout this book religiously!

Do all these things and I'm betting you will soon be published and for good money, and this is for whether you write science fiction, fantasy, or horror! I, for one, can't wait to welcome a new author into the fold. So good luck, as you embark on your new career as an author!

About The Author:

Rob Shelsky is an avid and eclectic writer, and averages about 4,000 words a day. Rob has two anthologies of dark science fiction, horror, and fantasy published, *Where Worlds Collide I*, and *Where Worlds Collide II*. He has several novels to his credit, three out now, *Verity*, a Regency Suspense Romance, the sequel, *Fallibility*, and *Lost Echoes*, a time-travel novel. Rob has written science fiction articles for such magazines as **The Internet Review of Science Fiction**, numerous articles for **AlienSkin Magazine, Neometropolis, Midnight Street (UK), Doorways**, and other publications.

Rob has had short stories published with **Jim Baen's Universe, Aberrant Dreams, AlienSkin, Gateway SF, Fifth Dimension, Continuum SF, Sonar4, Uncial Press, Planetary Stories, Pulp Spirit Magazine, Sex & Murder**, and many more. He has a novella coming out in the summer of 2011 with **Aberrant Dreams Magazine's** first hardcover edition anthology, *The Awakening*. Rob's novella, *Avenger Of The People*, will appear there alongside the works of such sci-fi greats as Alastair Reynolds, Ian Watson, Jana Oliver, Robert Madle, and just so many others. There is even an introduction by Jack McDevitt. The author has a short story, *Green Waters*, now out with **Sonar4's** *Phase Shift* anthology, and a paranormal story, *Light*

On The Moor, published as well. Other such genre stories include *The Crossroads Ghost*, and *A River Darkly*.

Now, Rob Shelsky is not only a writer, but an editor, as well as a contributing editor for **Currate.com** travel articles, and a reviewer for **Novelspot.**

Although widely traveled and continuing to travel, Rob now lives in North Carolina. He enjoys contemplating ideas for new stories while watching the sunsets over the hills and sipping a glass of red wine, preferably a decent Merlot.

APPENDIX—References

Science Fiction's Greatest Stolen Ideas

http://digg.com/arts_culture/Science_Fiction's_Greatest_Stolen_Ideas

Brainy Quote

http://www.brainyquote.com/quotes/authors/j/john_steinbeck.html

On having your ideas stolen by Howard Aiken

http://www.gurteen.com/gurteen/gurteen.nsf/id/X004EA36A/

Wikimedia

http://en.wikipedia.org/wiki/Steampunk

What Is Steampunk?

http://etheremporium.pbworks.com/What%20is%20Steampunk

What Is Steampunk? A Subculture Infiltrating Films, Music, Fashion, More

http://www.mtv.com/news/articles/1595812/20080926/abney_park.jhtml

Social Science 143 – Group 9

http://css-eng142-2009.wikispaces.com/Group+9

How William Shatner Changed The World

http://en.wikipedia.org/wiki/How_William_Shatner_Changed_the_World

Probing the limits of reality: the metaphysics in science fiction

http://www.iop.org/EJ/abstract/0031-9120/38/1/303

What is Sigma?

http://www.sigmaforum.org/